Chicago

Chicago, circa 1974: Laudir De Oliveira, Lee Loughnane, Peter Cetera, Walt Parazaider, Terry Kath, Danny Seraphine, James Pankow, Robert Lamm.

Chicago

Feelin' Stronger Every Day

BEN JOSEPH

QUARRY
MUSIC
BOOKS

Copyright © Ben Joseph, 2000.
All rights reserved.

The publisher acknowledges the support of
the Book Publishing Industry Development Program
of the Department of Canadian Heritage.

Chicago: Feelin' Stronger Every Day is a serious
critical and biographical study of the music and
career of the band Chicago. The quotation of
lyrics from songs written or performed by the
band illustrates the biographical and critical
information and analysis presented by the
author and thus constitutes fair use under
existing copyright conventions.

Order No. QP 00809
ISBN 1-55082-245-4

Chicago album cover collage and
book cover design by Susan Hannah.
Text photos from the private collection
of Joe Iaquinto, except for page 48,
courtesy of Kevin Knutsen, and page 108-109,
courtesy of Karen Simpson.
Typeset by Robert Stewart.

Printed in the United States of America by
Vicks Lithograph and Printing Corporation

Published by Quarry Press Inc,
PO Box 1061, Kingston, Ontario
K7L 4Y5 Canada,
www.quarrypress.com.

Exclusive Distributors:
Music Sales Corporation
257 Park Avenue South, New York, NY 10010 USA
Music Sales Limited
8/9 Frith Street, London W1D 3JB England
Music Sales Pty. Limited
120 Rothschild Street, Rosebery, Sydney, NSW 2018, Australia

CONTENTS

INTRODUCTION 7
BEGINNINGS 11

~

CHICAGO I 27
CHICAGO II 32
CHICAGO III 40
CHICAGO IV (Live at Carnegie Hall) 51
CHICAGO V 55
CHICAGO VI 61
CHICAGO VII 68
CHICAGO VIII 75
CHICAGO IX (Greatest Hits) 79
CHICAGO X 81
CHICAGO XI 86
CHICAGO XII (Hot Streets) 99
CHICAGO XIII 115
CHICAGO XIV 119
CHICAGO XV (Greatest Hits Vol. II) 123
CHICAGO XVI 126
CHICAGO XVII 136
CHICAGO XVIII .144
CHICAGO XIX 155
CHICAGO XX (Greatest Hits 1982-1989) 158
CHICAGO XXI 165
CHICAGO XXII (Stone of Sisyphus) 168
CHICAGO XXIII (Night and Day Big Band) 171
CHICAGO XXIV (The Heart of Chicago) 177
CHICAGO XXV (The Christmas Album) 179
CHICAGO XXVI (Live in Concert) 182

~

ACKNOWLEDGMENTS 186
SOURCES 187

FEELIN' STRONGER EVERY DAY

Chicago live at Madison Square Garden, 1976.

INTRODUCTION

> Hey there everybody
> Please don't romp or roam
> We're a little nervous
> 'Cause we're so far from home
>
> So this is what we do
> Sit back and let us groove
> And let us work on you...
> — Terry Kath, *Introduction*

Although I had listened to this song by Terry Kath opening the Chicago Transit Authority album many, many times on my record player at home, Terry Kath's voice was never so thrilling to my ears, his countenance to my eyes, as when the band took the stage at Madison Square Garden in 1975 during the legendary Beach Boys/Chicago tour that summer. The Beach Boys opened the show, sounding and looking just like their records, every face and every note a golden one, good vibrations emanating from the stage, but I could hardly keep from screaming, "Bring on Chicago." When Chicago took the stage, exuding a raw, nervous energy, I was transported to a rock and roll shangri-la. My musical heroes made the songs I had fallen in love with come to life with the intensity of a mystical experience. There they were, Terry Kath singing the beautiful *Make Me Smile*, Peter Cetera belting out *25 Or 6 To 4*, the rhythm and the horn sections more exciting than on record. I was a teenager seeing his favorite band for the first time. The experience proved to be momentous — I, too, would become a musician, inspired to do so by the music of Chicago. And Chicago would become and remain to this day the most successful American rock band of all time, next to their tour mates, The Beach Boys.

At the high school I attended in Brooklyn, New York, Chicago became a favorite of both school-band and the garage-band musicians. Arrangements of Chicago's songs were part of the repertoire for the stage band class because our teachers respected them as classically trained musicians who had crossed over into more popular rock — music a teacher could use to appeal to his hip students. If you were thinking about a career in music, Chicago was required learning. This band was living proof that a musical education was not an oxymoron. Chicago opened the door for a lot of young musicians who might have otherwise avoided brass and woodwinds in favor of guitars, bass, and drums in order to be accepted as cool, not that I did, taking up the bass as my instrument of choice. And that music also reached the same crowd that listened to Led Zeppelin and The Who and The Stones. Even if your garage band didn't have a horn section, you learned 25 Or 6 To 4. My garage band did happen to have a horn section, and we learned as much Chicago material as we could, performing it at dances and night clubs in New York throughout the 1970s, even embellishing some of the songs with disco grooves when the times changed.

Chicago became a musical 'crossover' phenomena, a rock band with horns, classically trained musicians who became rock legends and then were transformed again into pop stars in succession over a 30 year career, always respected as great musicians. In the early 1970s, well-respected and cutting-edge bands led by Buddy Rich and Maynard Ferguson were homing in on Chicago's sound and making it their own. Jazz guitar great Wes Montgomery recorded a version of *Does Anybody Really Know What Time It Is?* At the same time, famed conductor/arranger Andre Kostelanetz, sometimes credited for pioneering easy listening music, recorded an entire album of Chicago songs culled from the band's first three albums. The Russian-born Kostelanetz took *25 Or 6 To 4, It Better End Soon, Make Me Smile*, and eight other songs, reworked them for a full orchestra, and presented them to an audience that probably would have never listened to Chicago otherwise. According to the album's liner notes written by Mort Goode, "The Maestro was impressed by the music. The melodic feeling, the tempo, the structure. There was more than he imagined. Important material."

When the band changed gears in the 1980s, Chicago's celebrated power ballad sound practically became a blueprint for modern music. As the band mellowed with age, their work set the standard for the burgeoning Adult Contemporary genre. Rock bands like Journey and Heart followed their lead and found it to be quite lucrative. And with the bulk of the hit material becoming keyboard-oriented, throngs of piano players were busy learning the material. Top-40 bands throughout the world were belting out *You're The Inspiration*.

By the '90s, Chicago's sound had become ingrained in the musical

INTRODUCTION

landscape, their songs a part of the lexicon. Their influences could be heard in everything from source music to hit records by artists as diverse as Vanessa Williams and Green Day. In 1995, *Street Player* was sampled for the dance hit *The Bomb (These Sounds Fall Into My Mind)*, and in 1997, the twenty-something hip-hop group, Az Yet, hit big with their cover of *Hard To Say I'm Sorry*. A new generation was discovering Chicago and broadening the scope of their music.

Now, at the dawn of the 21st century, Chicago is entering their fifth decade by touring in support of their latest album, CHICAGO XXVI: LIVE IN CONCERT. The band has become one of the longest running acts in history and shows no signs of letting up. Whatever music comes out of this new decade, perhaps this new century, will undoubtedly contain trace elements of Chicago.

Chicago has now sold over 120 million records. They have released 26 albums, not counting imports and compilations. Five of their albums have reached Number One on the *Billboard* charts, while thirteen have gone platinum and twelve gold. Chicago ranks third behind The Beatles and The Rolling Stones for the group with the most Top 10 hits, according to *Billboard*. They have toured around the world again and again. Songs like *Beginnings*, *25 Or 6 To 4*, *Saturday in the Park*, and *If You Leave Me Now* are radio mainstays. Countless couples have danced at their weddings to *Colour My World*, *Just You 'N Me*, and *You're The Inspiration*. The band's vast body of work is *the* standard of classic American rock and pop music.

This book has been written as a tribute to Chicago's music and achievements. To begin my research for this book, I went back to my record collection and listened to Chicago's enormous body of work. While revisiting each album, I was quickly reminded how wonderful the music is. Along with this auditory journey, I broke out my Chicago video collection, donated by a friend, and re-lived wondrous concert experiences of the '60s, '70s, and '80s, as well as some of Chicago's rare television appearances. While the individual members of the band are not household names, their image as a 'band' is indelible. In the '60s, they looked like a '90s alternative rock act, grunge-style, all about music, not image. In the '70s, Chicago joined the ranks of the more flamboyant artists like Earth, Wind & Fire and Elton John with the horn section and Terry Kath often seen wearing capes and glitter outfits, while in the '80s Peter Cetera donned brightly colored jumpsuits and sported the latest Rock hair-do. Exhaustive research into reviews, articles, and press releases as well as interviews with key figures in the band's rich history round out this lifetime of admiration.

FEELIN' STRONGER EVERY DAY

Chicago has had a profound effect on my metier as a professional musician. They raised the bar for all of us. As a debt of gratitude, I am helping to nurture the next generation of fans by introducing my infant son to the band's music. So far he likes the Christmas album and all the songs with the word "baby" in them.

Chicago's legacy is undeniable. Their music will make you smile.

So . . . sit back and let us groove.

BEGINNINGS

Only the beginning
Of what I want to feel forever
Only the beginning
Only just the start . . .
— Robert Lamm, *Beginnings*

On February 15, 1967, in the basement of Walter Parazaider's parent's house in Chicago, six musicians — Lee Loughnane, Terry Kath, James Pankow, Danny Seraphine, Robert Lamm, and Paraziader himself — decided to form a "rock 'n' roll band with horns." While that idea may have seemed a bit odd at the time, it certainly wasn't that far-fetched. From the *Billboard* Top Singles and Album Charts for that particular week, it was quite evident that horn sections were being kept busy in recording studios throughout the world. Songs like *Happy Together* by the Turtles and *Penny Lane* by The Beatles featured prominent horn arrangements complimenting the vocals and helping to support the hooks and choruses. Hit records by R&B legends Stevie Wonder, The Temptations, and The Four Tops relied heavily on brass and woodwinds to enhance their grooves. Bands like Herb Alpert & the Tijuana Brass and Sergio Mendez & Brazil '66 used horn sections to help drive them up the charts.

What was far-fetched about these young musicians was the extent to which they would take their musical idea for a rock 'n' roll band with horns — the key words here being *rock 'n' roll*. While The Beatles and the Turtles may have hired outside horn sections to play on their records, they were by no means part of the band. Walter Parazaider on sax, James Pankow on trombone, Lee Loughnane on trumpet, Danny Seraphine on drums, Terry Kath on guitar and vocals, and Robert Lamm on keyboards, key bass, and vocals started a band whose horn section was an integral, symbiotic part of the group, front and center on the stage. Initially calling themselves The Music Foundation, they quickly changed their name to The Big Thing, a somewhat uninspired choice of name as Parazaider explains. "An Italian friend of mine who was going to book us said, 'You know, everybody is saying *Thing! Thing this, Thing that.* There's a lot of you. We'll call you *The Big Thing.*'" The newly formed Big Thing played its first engagement at the GiGi A Go Go in Lyons, Illinois, in March 1967, but by the end of the year, they had chosen the truly inspired name Chicago Transit Authority, taking the words from the city's transportation system and thus making Chicago the band and Chicago the city synonymous, even though they had now moved to Los Angeles to record, where they soon truly became a big thing.

Their inspiration to form a rock 'n' roll band with horns came from their musical training, though the members of the band have musical backgrounds quite different from most rock musicians. While most the rock stars of the 1960s credited rockabilly or rhythm and blues as the source of their inspiration — music icons like Elvis, Little Richard, Fats Domino, Chuck Berry, and Buddy Holly — Walter Parazaider, for example, had other role models. "I started playing when I was nine years old because I saw Benny Goodman on *The Ed Sullivan Show*," he recalls. "I was a clarinetist to start with." Born in Chicago on March 14, 1945 Walt's formal music training began when he was nine. He studied the clarinet and other reeds at age eleven, and began learning the saxophone when he was thirteen. At this early age, his primary goal was to play in a big band because his father had been a member of Woody Herman's orchestra. Parazaider inherited his interest in music from his father who had given up performing full time to play part time when he began his family. "I can't think of a time growing up when there wasn't music in the house," Parazaider says, "whether it was my dad practicing by himself or playing in a band that was rehearsing at the house, or my mother listening to records. And that's from my earliest recollection." By the time he reached his early teens, Walter became a proficient player and the protege of the E-flat clarinetist in the Chicago Symphony Orchestra.

The popular music of the late 1950s soon began to have an influence on Parazaider, however. "I picked up the saxophone along the way," Parazaider recalls, "and discovered that you could make a buck, and get some girls, playing a saxophone in a rock 'n' roll band. So, I enjoyed a 'schizoid' musical existence, so to speak, from about the age of thirteen on, playing in anything from an octet, playing all the standard big band tunes, and rock 'n' roll, from *Tequila*, to any of the Ventures stuff that they'd use a saxophone on. I did that along with pursuing the classical career, because my aspiration at that time was to take my teacher's place in the Chicago symphony." To pursue this goal,

BEGINNINGS

Parazaider then enrolled at Chicago's DePaul University, where his teacher from the Chicago Symphony was on staff, but to study education, not music. During this 'schizoid' period, he was playing "many gigs and smoke-filled rooms and dance halls," he explains, "and also some orchestra balls," which, if nothing else, convinced him to become a professional musician. "After about a year and a half of realizing I didn't want to study trigonometry and how to teach health class in school, and also realizing, with the help of some of my professors, that because I wasn't a patient person, I wasn't cut out to be a teacher, I changed my major. I prepared for about a year and a half and played a degree recital for the principal members of the Chicago Symphony and an audience. I passed with flying colors and received a playing degree in orchestral clarinet. In the meantime, I had taken all my Master's credits in English Lit."

While Walt was attending DePaul University, he met another young Chicago musician, Jimmy Guercio, who further down the road became Chicago's producer. "We started playing in different rock 'n' roll bands in the area," Parazaider recalls. "We played a lot of the beer bashes at Northwestern University and the surrounding colleges in the area, and we became quite friendly."

While at DePaul, Parazaider had also developed a new musical idea, far removed from classical music, that he thought had great possibilities: horns integrated with rock 'n' roll. As trends in pop music always tend to fluctuate, the popularity of big-band horns waned in the mid-1960s. During that period, many groups took refuge in mimicking the four-piece rhythm section format of popular bands like the early Beatles and The Rolling Stones, working within the confines of two guitars, bass, and drums. Even the saxophone, a crucial part of fifties rock 'n' roll, was heard less frequently. James Brown and a few other R&B artists were the only people in the charts who perpetuated the big-band tradition. But then in the summer of 1966, the Beatles turned it all around and reintroduced horns to the Top 10. Their *Revolver* album featured songs such as *Got To Get You Into My Life*," which included two trumpets and two tenor saxophones, a radical approach for 1966 chart toppers. All of these musical influences and trends were studied by Walter Parazaider and introduced to his first band, The Missing Links.

The bass player for The Missing Links was a very talented musician named Terry Kath. Kath, who was born in Chicago on January 31, 1946, had been a friend of Parazaider's and Guercio's from their teens. By the time he was in the eighth grade, Kath had developed an affinity for his older brother's drum set,

FEELIN' STRONGER EVERY DAY

which he played for a year. He then gravitated to his mother's banjo, which he retuned to play like a guitar. A year or so later, Kath eventually got a hold of his first guitar and amplifier and started his first band, The Mystics. The five-piece teenage rock band, inspired by The Ventures, played their share of dances, clubs, and VFW halls. Kath, already a commanding presence on the instrument, would cause the dancers to stop in their tracks and listen. After recording some of their songs at a local studio and taking up with The Buckinghams management, Kath left The Mystics and began playing with Jimmy Rice and the Gentleman and thereby with Walter Parazaider. The band recorded a record for Louis Prima's 'record label. Achieving no commercial success there, Kath and Parazaider moved on to Jimmy Ford and the Executives, which led to their road work with the Dick Clark Show. Kath, who had played the upright bass in high school, bought a Fender Jazz Bass and joined the Dick Clark tour as a bassist. He continued playing bass and eventually formed The Missing Links with drummer Danny Seraphine. After three or four months, he switched back to the guitar.

As for Terry's early influences, there was a lot of jazz on his turntable. As Kath once told *Guitar Player Magazine*, "After the Ventures, I dug Johnny Smith quite a bit. And George Benson, when he was with Brother Jack McDuff. I heard him with saxophonist Stanley Turrentine and he really knocked me out. I listened to a lot of Kenny Burrell when I was starting, too. And Howard Roberts, man. I had all of Howard's albums. Mike Bloomfield's 'East/West' was a fine record. I used to sit around the house all the time and play guitar with it." Kath mentioned that he also liked Eric Clapton's playing on the FRESH CREAM album. "But then there was Hendrix, man," continues Kath. "Jimi was really the last cat to freak me. Jimi was playing all the stuff I had in my head. I couldn't believe it, when I first heard him. Man, no one can ever do what he did with a guitar. No one can ever take his place."

Although he was primarily self-taught, Kath did study for a year, taking lessons from Chicago area studio musician, Stu Pierce. "He just kept wanting me to play good lead stuff," Kath recalls, "but then all I wanted to do was play those rock and roll chords." It has been said that Terry Kath could not read music, but that wasn't the case. Fellow Mystics bandmate Brian Higgins, who studied with Pierce as well, sheds some light on that misconception. "Terry could read music in a basic way." Higgins claims that Kath could not read music as complex as Chicago's, but that he learned it by ear.

Trumpet player Lee Loughnane, also a DePaul student, frequently sat in

BEGINNINGS

with the band. Loughnane was born in Chicago on October 21, 1946. "My dad was a product of the Swing Era," he recalls. "He was a bandleader in the Army Air Force in World War I." In that capacity, Chief Warrant Officer Loughnane played trumpet with some of the top players from the big bands of the era who had been drafted. But he also came in contact with their lifestyles."My dad knew that they were only going to be with him for a certain amount of time, and then they were going to get shipped out to the front lines," says Loughnane. "So, he was a little more lax in his discipline than he might have been under other circumstances. Some of the guys would go AWOL on weekends to play gigs in town and then, come back drunk or high on something, and my dad would cover for them. As a result, he gained a dislike for drugs and alcohol, and when he left the army, he left the music behind. The only thing he brought home was his trumpet, which was the first one that I used. I had never heard him play." At age eleven, Loughnane attempted to play that trumpet. Lee began taking trumpet lessons when he was in seventh grade. He had no interest in rock until late in high school. In fact, Lee used to love to play along with Glenn Miller and Tommy Dorsey records during his youth. He had trouble identifying with rock because the only brass instrument found in pop at the time was the saxophone. He enrolled at St. Mel's High School rather than St. Patrick's, even though St. Patrick's was much closer to his home, because St. Mel's had a concert band, a jazz band, and a marching band. In addition, the band director, Tom Fabish, was the same band director who had taught Loughnane's father when he was in high school.

Loughnane knew that he wanted to be a professional musician when he graduated from high school in 1964. "There was nothing else that I wanted to do," he recalls. "I had no other calling. . . . Tom Fabish was also the band director at DePaul University, so when I got ready to enroll in college, it was the perfect school. Tom, my dad, and I decided that if I was intent upon a career in music, I should get a teaching degree for insurance, just in case my lofty plans at success as a professional musician didn't pan out." But, as with Parazaider, it didn't work out that way. "I loved the music classes, but I didn't so much love the general education classes that I had to take in order to get that kind of degree," Loughnane says, "and I would get to the point where I just wouldn't go to those classes." Lee studied for two years at DePaul University, in addition to his private instruction under John Nuzzo. This he followed with one year under Joe Summerhill at the Chicago Conservatory College.

Like other future members of Chicago, Loughnane began his career by performing in local groups. His first band was the Shannon Show Band, an Irish group where he was part of a trio horn section comprised of trumpet, trombone, and tenor saxophone — exactly the format *Chicago* would use. When the band wasn't working, he would play an occasional Italian festival, a Chicago State Street parade, or a wedding. Loughnane also worked with another band during this period called Ross and the Majestics, who became the house band during the summer in a bar in the basement of the Palmer House, a chic Chicago hotel. By accepting this gig, Loughnane had to quit a summer job his father had obtained for him on the graveyard shift at the Revere Copper and Brass Company. "Dad and I disagreed on my decision to take the job with Ross, but that was the band at the time, and I couldn't let them down." Loughnane's dislike of manual labor was reinforced after enduring another summer job at the Chicago State Hospital. "I knew that playing the trumpet was a lot more fun and definitely easier on the back," he says. Towards the end of that summer he decided to set out on his own. "I went out and got an apartment, and then I met Terry."

After Terry Kath introduced Loughnane to Danny Seraphine and Walter Parazaider, he began to sit in and jam with The Missing Links. Parazaider, Kath, Seraphine, and Loughnane then decided to develop Parazaider's concept of a rock 'n' roll band with horns. In order to make this plan materialize; they needed to find additional band members. In the fall of 1966, Parazaider approached a newly transferred DePaul sophomore trombone player from Quincy College. "Walt had been kind of keeping an eye on me in school," recalls James Pankow. "He approached me and said, 'Hey, man, I've been checking you out, and I like your playing, and I think you got it.' I said, well, what do you mean, 'I got it?' He had that twinkle in his eye, and I figured, well, whatever the hell he means, I guess he likes what I do."

Born in St. Louis, Missouri, on August 20, 1947, James Pankow had certainly spent enough time with his instrument by that point to know his chops. "I was in fifth grade, and my folks realized that I was a human beat box," he says. James has an impressive musical background. His interest in music developed while he was playing trombone in grammar- and high-school bands. While majoring in music at Quincy College in Illinois, he became interested in jazz and formed his own jazz quintet. While a student, James worked with several big bands, including the Bobby Christian and Ted Weems Orchestras and Bill Rosso's Chicago Jazz Ensemble. "It was good experience playing with a big band," he recalls. "However, I wasn't really learning

BEGINNINGS

anything creative because the music was passe."

In order to have the freedom in which to experiment, Pankow formed his own group at DePaul University. He began writing simpler, more modern songs. While he was there, he came into contact with many of the musicians who would later form Chicago and he discovered that their goals were mutual. James felt the framework of Chicago has given him the impetus to expand his creativity, something which might be lacking if they were all to work separately. "The possibilities available to us have helped me realize I have the potential to be creative. Everyone in this group is a dedicated musician," he reflects. "Everyone in this group is able to work together to create the sound we all want." Pankow credits the most important factor in Chicago's success as the group's brotherly closeness, which created a sense of mutual respect. "Music is the greatest emotional release there is," Pankow remarks. "In my songs, I hope to influence the mass of people in order to make the world a happier place. In a very sad, very frightened world, I know that I personally feel close to home through music."

Pankow's induction brought the new band's supplement of horns up to three, but they still needed to find bass and keyboard players. They thought they had gotten lucky in a bar on the South Side when they heard piano player 'Bobby Charles' of Bobby Charles and the Wanderers, whose given name was Robert Lamm. Lamm was born in Brooklyn, New York, on October 13, 1944, and, like Pankow, seemed to be infatuated with music even when he was a baby. "I was interested in music from the time I was a toddler," he says. "Both my mother and father were collectors of jazz records, and there always seemed to be music playing at our house." Lamm's mother encouraged him to join a Brooklyn Heights Choir; his first formal music training began there. He began playing the piano at that point, and discovered that he could sit down and play songs by ear. When Lamm was fifteen, his mother decided to re-marry and the family moved to Chicago. In Chicago he soon met other ambitious high school musicians and together they started a band. Lamm studied with the prominent jazz teacher Millie Collins. His musical icon became Ray Charles, who both wrote and played, and Lamm named himself after his champion. "I was writing songs in a band or two before Chicago," he recalls, "the dubious quality of which is another discussion. Writing songs wasn't yet the all-consuming passion it is now." The Bobby Charles and the Wanderers' solid blues foundation and the Ray Charles influences earned the band a wide popularity at dance halls and nightclubs. When Bobby Charles and the Wanderers broke up, Robert

FEELIN' STRONGER EVERY DAY

began to pursue the fascination he had held for keyboard instruments since the days when he was a choirboy. Before entering college, he concentrated his attentions on jazz piano.

While he was becoming an active part of the Chicago music scene, Robert attended the Music School at Roosevelt University, studying piano and composition. It was during these months at Roosevelt University that he became involved with other members of what was to become Chicago. One afternoon, Lamm got a phone call from one of the group forming Chicago: he doesn't remember exactly who called him, but the voice on the other end of the phone sketched out the ideas of starting a band that could perform rock 'n' roll with horns in it and asked if Robert was interested. He replied that he was. He was also asked if he knew how to play the bass pedals on an organ, which would compensate for finding a bass player for the band. "I lied and told them I could," he says. "I needed to learn how to do it real quick, and I did, on the job."

Robert met the other guys in the band at a meeting set up to resolve how to put their musical ideas into action. The date was February 15, 1967. "We had a get-together in Walter's apartment on the north side of Chicago," says Pankow. "It was Danny, Terry, Robert, Walter, Lee, and myself, and we agreed to devote our lives and our energies to making this project work." The group rehearsed in Parazaider's parents' basement as frequently as they could. "We figured that the only people with horn sections that were really making any noise were the soul acts," says Pankow, "so we kind of became a soul band doing James Brown and Wilson Pickett stuff."

Although Robert Lamm quickly learned to play bass on the organ, the band soon decided to add an electric bass guitar player to the mix. Bass player Peter Cetera was born in Chicago on September 13, 1944. His first instrument was the accordion, which he began to play when he was ten. "That's unfortunately true," he admits, when asked about it. "There was accordion and guitar, and for some reason I chose accordion. I don't know why. I guess because I was half-Polish, and we played a lot of polkas. It didn't do me any good for my rock 'n' roll career, but it actually was a lot of fun." His serious musical career began a couple of years later. "I started listening to music," he recalls, "and when I was a sophomore in high school, I bought a little guitar from Sears and started singing at the school functions. I met a senior who played guitar, and we started singing together." He said, 'Let's start a group,' and I said, 'Fine, I'll buy a bass.' We played all the Homecoming dances and all the weekend dances, doing Top 40 material. My senior year,

BEGINNINGS

I got together with the Exceptions. I stuck with them for five or six years."

Cetera was the answer to a prayer as far as the musical needs of The Big Thing. "We needed a bass player at the time," notes Loughnane. "Robert was playing the bass pedals on the organ. He did a pretty good job, but there just wasn't enough bottom with the bass pedals. You needed a real bass in the band. And we needed a tenor voice. We had two baritones (Lamm and Kath), so we had midrange and lower notes covered. But we needed a high voice for the same reason that you have three horns. You have trumpet, tenors, and trombone. You cover as much range harmonically as you can, and we wanted to do the same thing vocally. When Peter joined the band that solidified our vocals. You could get more color, musically, and we started building from there."

The drummer for The Big Thing was Danny Seraphine. Born in Chicago on August 28, 1948, he grew up in the Little Italy section of Chicago. Inspired by his uncle who was a drummer and played at family gatherings, Seraphine began playing drums at the age of nine. By the time he was twelve, he was playing in numerous rock bands. He met Walt Parazaider and Terry Kath at an audition for a group called The Executives when he was fifteen. While Danny was studying percussion with Bob Tilles, a well-known percussion genius at DePaul University, he began gigging with several musicians from The Missing Links. After Danny left DePaul University, he continued his studies under the tutelage of Chuck Flores, who had worked with Maynard Ferguson and Woody Herman's bands. "I like to study music even now," he explains. "It keeps me going and causes me to progress. And then when we used to go to New York and record (some of our early records were done in New York), I got connected with Papa Joe Jones, probably the all-time greatest brush player. I studied with him whenever we were in New York. So I was really in that mode for a long time, and it really obviously helped develop my technique." Danny's influences are as diverse as his style. They include Buddy Rich, Tony Williams, Mitch Mitchell, Elvin Jones, and Grady Tate. However, he points out, "I still try to maintain my own direction. I have learned that the great musicians have mastered a variety of musical forms in order for them to have a complete understanding of music itself."

As the band developed in Chicago under the name of The Big Thing, the group realized that continued progression would not be possible in the city

FEELIN' STRONGER EVERY DAY

of Chicago. Because of the social climate at the time, people in clubs and dances were not receptive to the group's efforts to broaden musical horizons. The band felt they were approaching a dead end in the city where they began. "As our style began to change, " recalls Walt Parazaider, "it became evident that we would have to come to Los Angeles." James William Guercio, the record producer who had pulled together The Big Thing, also encouraged the move to the LA music scene. Guercio brought the group to California and changed their name to Chicago Transit Authority in honor of the bus line he used to ride on to school. He moved the band members into a small two-bedroom house near the Hollywood Freeway and told them not to worry about anything but their music. As James Pankow recalls, "We made the move in June of 1968. We threw all of our lives in U-haul trailers and drove across the country. The married guys left their wives at home at first because they couldn't afford to bring their families out. We got disturbance calls from the neighbors five times a day because all we did was practice day and night." Chicago Transit Authority soon began to gig in the Los Angeles area. "I think we made all of $15, $20 at whatever beer hall we could play in the suburbs of Los Angeles for a while there," says Parazaider.

Chicago Transit Authority was not the first rock band with horns that Guercio had produced. Previously, he had made a deal with Columbia Records to sign The Buckinghams. A quintet formerly know as The Pulsations, The Buckinghams began in Chicago in 1965 and had a string of local singles before they received national airplay with *Kind of a Drag*, a pop song arranged with horns that topped the charts in February '67. Later that year, Guercio produced a series of hits for Columbia, including one he co-wrote, *Susan*. It was at this point that Guercio was approached to work with Blood, Sweat & Tears (BS&T), which at the time was called The Blues Project, led by Al Kooper. As Guercio explains, "I met with the Blues Project's manager, Sid Bernstein, and Al Kooper. Al said, 'I've got to put this jazz-rock band together with horns in it, and I'm using some of the guys in The Blues Project. The Buckinghams is kind of what I want to do. You're the best. You understand horns. You can write charts. You're a musician." But Guercio couldn't do the project because he had an exclusive contract for The Buckinghams with CBS Records president Clive Davis, and Bernstein was locked into Atlantic Records. There was another reason for Guerico's reticence with Al Kooper. Guerico explained to Al, "I said, 'Al, I'm bringing all these players together. I'm gonna do the first horn band. I can't do yours.' Six months later, I hear they're signed to CBS! They never

BEGINNINGS

got the deal at Atlantic, and John Simon's doing them, and that was Blood, Sweat & Tears' first album, CHILD IS FATHER TO THE MAN. And I'm goin', 'Oh, shit.'"

The Buckinghams' string of hits was already history in June 1968 when a drug bust put an end to their national career. By that time Guercio felt his old college mates from Chicago were ready to go forward with the 'rock-plus-horns' concept. Guercio also believed in what James Pankow calls his dream: "To make the city of Chicago and Chicago's artists and talent a focal point and bring music from the Midwest to the rest of the world, instead of giving all the credit to Los Angeles and New York."

"We ran into Jimmy Guercio," recalls Parazaider, "who happened to be in Chicago at the time, passing through on a tour or something like that, or going on to New York to do The Buckinghams' record, and he came out to Niles, Michigan, and he heard us play. He was very impressed, and if I had to point to one thing, you know, everybody says that they need a break, and they have to recognize it and jump on it when they see it. Jimmy Guercio was our break because he was a producer at Columbia who was putting a Buckinghams' record together that was gonna become a very successful record. He said, 'Hang on, and I'll be in touch with you. I'll be coming in from time to time to check on your progress.' As Pankow recalls, "he said, 'Just keep doing what you're doing, and I'll be back.' We didn't know what to think other than, 'Hey, man, this guy must know what he's talking about. He didn't do too bad with The Buckinghams. So, let's get our act together and research some more original material, see what our potential is.' So, we developed more original material. I began to write songs. Robert began to write more songs, and Terry Kath began to contribute material."

"I think we were playing a couple of songs that were original," says Lamm. "There's a tune called *Mississippi Delta City Blues* Terry Kath wrote that ended up on the eleventh album. *Wake Up Sunshine* which appeared on CHICAGO III, and another song called *Dedicated To Girl Number One*, which I think is the first thing that Guercio recorded, kind of as a demo, to see how it would be, how to go about recording this band, something that he recorded with us in L.A. long before we ever got into the studio to do the CHICAGO TRANSIT AUTHORITY album. We wrote and rehearsed at constant writing and rehearsal seminars, and all of this material was what was to become CHICAGO TRANSIT AUTHORITY, the first album." "When you think about it," adds Parazaider, "the first three albums, that were double albums, and especially the first two, we had enough material for two double albums by the time we ever set foot in the studio for the CHICAGO TRANSIT AUTHORITY album."

Their song writing abilities also expanded during these early months. From the start, Robert Lamm was a key songwriter for the group and the most politically active member. However, he is quick to point out he speaks only for himself and doesn't presume to say he is expressing the views of the band. "When I compose a song concerning the social and political climate, I am simply expressing my own beliefs, even if no one else in the group agrees with what I am saying. I feel I have a responsibility to be honest with those who listen to my music. In writing songs, I must write what I am thinking about, because so far I have found it unsatisfying to compose a fictional lyric idea." Robert's beliefs become evident in tunes such as *Dialogue* and *State of the Union* on Chicago's fifth album, for example. Robert has worked consistently to bring his social concerns into action. He has done many radio spots to encourage voter registration and the need to use, assertively, the power of the vote. Robert composed and recorded the song *Where You Think You're Going?* to discourage addictive drug abuse, making it available to all radio stations, and later did a film version of the song for television.

"I'm not sure exactly what led me to the realization that I could write about things other than romantic topics," Lamm says. "I think just being alive in those times and watching that conflict in Asia unfold on television daily, because Lord knows we all sat around and watched a lot of television, then the culture shock of moving from Chicago to California. And then the alternative press — the *L.A. Free Press* — was very much into the hot topic of revolution. It seemed that the generation of which I was a member, and the generation which was forming the new bands, had a connection. So it seemed natural to give voice to some of the thinking. As pinheaded (he laughs) as some of my opinions and those of some of my contemporaries may have been at the time, it felt really real. It felt like it was right, it was right that a lot of bands at the time were giving voice to the idea of the average person having a certain amount of power, and power, maybe enough, to stand up to the policies of the government and protest the war." Lamm's will to put his beliefs into action has shaped the character of Chicago as a conscientious band.

"In the meantime, we were working as an opening act at the Whisky A-Go-Go and college bars and other rock 'n' roll clubs in the LA area," says Pankow, "and by word of mouth, we started becoming the new sensation in LA. It started happening all over again. Jimmy Guercio figured that the

BEGINNINGS

Whisky would be a great springboard for people in the record industry to hear us, and, indeed, through those engagements Jimmy Guercio was able to negotiate a contract with CBS."

In his 1974 autobiography, *Clive: Inside The Record Business*, ex-CBS Records president Clive Davis tells a story about the signing of Chicago Transit Authority to Columbia Records. Davis says that he received a telephone call from David Geffen, who was an agent at the time, praising the group, and that he waited for Guercio to bring them in, since Guercio had a contract giving Columbia first look at all his artists until the label selected three, and two of those — Firesign Theatre and Illinois Speed Press — had already been signed. But when Guercio did come calling, with producer Mike Curb in tow, he tried to sell Davis on The Arbors, a group CBS had dropped from a subsidiary label months before. Davis then insisted he would turn down every suggestion until Chicago Transit Authority was on the table.

Guercio disputes that statement completely. He has a much more involved story to tell." I had invested all of my dollars in keeping this band Chicago Transit Authority alive," he says. "It probably created the seeds of resentment. It was so tough. I took them out of making $200 a night. I had moved them to California, and I knew they were my best project. The group does not know the struggle. I was beating the shit out of them in rehearsals. 'I don't like this tune.' 'Change the structure.' 'This isn't good enough.' And they were just playing bars. It was very tough. I wasn't real polite about it, 'cause we didn't have much time, and it wasn't an easy thing to do. So, you create a lot of resentment."

When Guercio thought the band was ready, he showcased them for CBS at the Whisky on August 19, 1968. The label's West Coast A&R department turned Chicago Transit Authority down. According to the terms of the contract, the label was allowed three opportunities to see each act, and this was strike one. Later in late September, they were turned down again. It is perhaps worth pausing to consider Guercio's position vis-a-vis CBS at this time, since it seems simultaneously close and somewhat adversarial, and would continue to be. Today, independent producers are an accepted fact of life in the record industry. But in 1968, producers were usually employed by record labels, and worked only in studios also owned by the labels. Guercio may have worked exclusively for CBS, but he was an early maverick. "I was an independent producer," he explains. "I was not allowed to exist. It was like being the lowest form of life on the planet. These staff producers all had overhead, American

FEELIN' STRONGER EVERY DAY

Express cards, limos, salaries, and a small percentage. They all looked down on me. There were a couple that got along with me. They all hated my guts because I was making a fortune. I had everything signed to me personally, then I leased it to CBS."

But Guercio also had certainly demonstrated an ability to deliver hits, especially with a horn band, which may help explain the remarkable turn of events that now ensued. Blood, Sweat & Tears had released its debut album, CHILD IS FATHER TO THE MAN, to only moderate sales, and had then gone through a reorganization during which Al Kooper was ousted and singer David Clayton-Thomas was in. Now they were preparing to record their second album, and Guercio was approached to produce the album at what Guercio recalls as an outrageous Hollywood party, during which Janis Joplin brained Jim Morrison with a liquor bottle. "Bennett Glotzer (BS&T's manager) is following me around saying, 'You gotta produce Blood, Sweat & Tears,'" Guercio explains. "I said, 'The first album's a stiff, I've already got a horn band, give me a break!' Alan wanted me to do the first project. He says, 'You've gotta do it. It's a new band. We've got this Canadian singer, David Clayton-Thomas. You gotta come back to New York. You gotta see it.' I made it so difficult because I was running out of money, and I was getting turned down by CBS. I said, 'Listen. These son-of-a-bitches have just turned down my group at two showcases.' He says, 'I can get anything you want.' I said, 'You get me a studio, you get me a hotel room at the Drake Hotel for as many months as I want it. You pay for all my plane tickets. I commute to L.A. every weekend. I fly in for four days. You get this band rehearsed, and I'll think about it. Call me Monday.' And that's what happened. They rolled out the red carpet, and they really were pissed off about it, but Bennett pulled it off. Nobody ever talked to me. Nobody ever put a 'purchase order' in front of me. All of a sudden, from being turned down, not being able to get one penny out of CBS, not being able to get studio time, I got carte blanche if I'd do Blood, Sweat & Tears."

Though he was doing the project primarily to continue funding Chicago Transit Authority and to find a way to get them signed to CBS, Guercio was still faced with the problem of explaining his apparent defection to the group. "Jimmy called me up, and he asked me to ask the other guys, 'Would it be okay if he did the Blood, Sweat & Tears second album,'" Parazaider recalls. "At first I was going, 'Well, jeez, man, that's horns and what's going on?' and I voiced that opinion to him. He says, 'To tell you the truth, I really haven't recorded horns as a whole band situation. I've recorded horns that did sort of 'blaps' here

BEGINNINGS

and there, or little parts here and there. This would be a good way for me to learn how to record horns.' I don't think it was lip service, because he really hadn't recorded horns per-se. He has some background horns, and we were basically a band with integrated horns in the band, not as backup horns. I have to believe him on this because, if you think about it, what the horn section did, from the start, was a lot different than Blood, Sweat & Tears, and the sound was copied many times over after we got 'the *Chicago* horn sound.' So, I think with Blood, Sweat & Tears the horns were recorded in a much different way than Chicago's horns were. Of course, if you look at the two bands, you would say that they were really a jazz-rock 'n' roll band where we were, they called us a jazz-rock band after Blood, Sweat & Tears faded away, but we were basically a 'rock 'n' roll band with horns'."

"Terry was really pissed off," says Guercio. "I said, 'Terry, there ain't even a guitar player in this band. On top of it, I'm using studio players, and I'm only doin' it three, four days a week. Let's get this shit together. We'll blow 'em off the stage. Don't worry about it.' So, I'm flying back to New York, and I made the most antiseptic record you could ever make, but I thought it was pretty good. But I had a very tough time, and those guys really don't like me, 'cause I was just there for one album. Bennett got me everything I needed, and I felt there was a tacit agreement that I'd get a chance to record Chicago immediately after that."

The problem was that the tacit agreement didn't seem to be getting any closer to a signed contract. This, according to Guercio, is where Mike Curb, also an independent producer in Los Angeles at the time, stepped in. "I called Mike up," Guercio says. "Mike was the only guy that would help me. He had a little demo studio. I said, 'Listen, CBS has turned them down. I'm having a big problem with Clive Davis. I'm going to do Blood, Sweat & Tears, and it's going to be a hit, but they turned down Chicago again, and I've got to record them. I'm running out of money'. He says, 'I'll record 'em'. So everybody went in, and we did a demo for Mike Curb (this is the record Robert Lamm remembers), and Clive heard about it, which I knew he would do. Mike immediately started touting it everywhere. The minute Mike had an interest and started calling everybody, saying 'There's this incredible band that Jimmy's recording, I let 'em in my studio, listen to this,' CBS changes their position."

From the New York studio where he was producing Blood, Sweat & Tears, Guercio was summoned to Davis' office. "Chicago gets signed with CBS because Clive insists that it was a mistake by the California A&R department, that they never should have turned Chicago down, and he always wanted Chicago," Guercio says, though he doesn't believe the explanation he received. Rather, he has his own theory. "He (Davis) was trying to break me," Guercio says. "And he ended up doing it. Chicago's entire advance was $5,000 when Clive eventually caved in."

Through a series of sophisticated maneuvers, Guercio had managed to get Chicago Transit Authority signed to Columbia Records, with recording sessions scheduled to begin in January, seven months after arriving in California, almost two years since they had formed in Parazaider's Chicago apartment.

CHICAGO I

CHICAGO TRANSIT AUTHORITY

CG8

Daniel Seraphine (drums) ᴧᴧ James Pankow (trombone) ᴧᴧ Peter Cetera (bass and lead vocals) ᴧᴧ Walter Parazaider (woodwinds and background vocals) ᴧᴧ Lee Loughnane (trumpet and background vocals) ᴧᴧ Terry Kath (guitar and lead vocals) ᴧᴧ Robert Lamm (keyboard and lead vocals)

Side 1
Introduction
Does Anybody Really Know What Time It Is?
Beginnings

Side 2
Questions 67 and 68
Listen
Poem 58

Side 3
Free Form Guitar
South California Purples
I'm A Man

Side 4
Prologue, August 29, 1968
Someday (August 29, 1968)
Liberation

The historic debut album CHICAGO TRANSIT AUTHORITY was recorded over a period of eleven days, from January 20 to 30, 1969, at CBS Studios in New York City. While the band was in the studio working on this seminal album, artists like Marvin Gay, Stevie Wonder, The Supremes, and B.J. Thomas were topping the *Billboard* charts and radio playlists with hits like *For Once In My Life*, *Hooked on a Feeling*, and *Love Child*. Young-Holt Unlimited scored big with the instrumental *Soulful Strut*. All those records featured orchestration and horn sections, prominent in the mix and crucial to the overall sound and ultimate success of the songs. At the same time, rock music was starting to receive more attention in the charts with albums by Steppenwolf, Jimi Hendrix, Janis Joplin, Cream, and Iron Butterfly riding high into the summer of Woodstock.

When CHICAGO TRANSIT AUTHORITY was released in 1969, it seemed to be the perfect synthesis of everything that was diametrically opposed. Smooth, lush harmonies, distorted feedback-drenched guitars, Beatles-meet-Motown

FEELIN' STRONGER EVERY DAY

bass work, Buddy Rich-meets-Mitch Mitchell drums, churning Hammond organ, classical piano, and those powerful horns weaving in and out of the arrangements, ending up toe-to-toe with everything else. And it all worked. The dynamics were perfect. This 'rock 'n' roll band with horns' came into the world kicking and screaming.

Taking a cue from The Beatles WHITE ALBUM, CTA was a double record. The band had amassed such a high volume of material it was a logical step, though CBS did not exactly agree and they forced the group to trim their royalties. Terry Kath captured the essence of the band with his *Introduction*, which, appropriately enough, opened the album. The song featured the band playing over time changes, sophisticated chord progressions, and moving seamlessly through each new phase of the tune, which migrated from 'arena rock' to soft jazz and back again. Kath, who also sang lead on the track, let the world know just how grateful the band was to be where they were: "With heaven's help we blended, and we do thank the Lord." Truer words were never spoken. Chicago Transit Authority, or Chicago, as the liner notes suggested we call them, seemed to have everything in the right place. The horn section, the vocalists, and the rhythm section were tight and unified. Individually, the members of Chicago were all outstanding on their respective instruments. Unlike many bands of the era that utilized session musicians for their recordings, Chicago was completely self-contained.

Out of the twelve tunes on the album, Robert Lamm penned seven, including what would become one of Chicago's most endearing songs, *Beginnings*. Lamm wrote *Beginnings* after visiting the legendary LA club, The Ash Grove, upon his arrival in LA. Folk legend Richie Havens was performing and, according to Lamm, provided the inspiration for the song.

> When I'm with you
> It doesn't matter where we are
> Or what we're doing
> I'm with you, that's all that matters
>
> Time passes much too quickly
> When we're together laughing
> I wish I could sing it to you
> Oh, oh, I wish I could sing it to you
> — Robert Lamm, *Beginnings* (ASCAP)

CHICAGO I

Side two of the album opened with Lamm's *Questions '67 and '68*. Released as a single, the song featured blistering fusion-tinged guitar leads by Kath and introduced the soaring tenor voice of bassist Peter Cetera. Chicago's vocal prowess set them far apart from so many other groups who have come and gone. That amazing blend that Kath spoke of was definitely heaven-sent, as Chicago was blessed with three vocalists who could cover the entire spectrum.

Three more songs by Lamm — *Listen, Poem 58,* and *South California Purples* — should have been enough to convince anyone that Chicago was decidedly more rock than jazz. But if there were any skeptics left, they had to have been convinced by the end of Terry Kath's 6:53 *Free Form Guitar*, which was basically Kath brutalizing a Fender Stratocaster a la Hendrix. The liner notes went so far as to explain how the track was recorded and what equipment was used.

James Pankow, who would soon write some of Chicago's biggest and best remembered classic hits, supplied the last two songs on side four. *Someday (August 29, 1968)*, which he co-wrote with Robert Lamm, was a bouncy, protest song, sung by Lamm and Cetera. The song announced that "the end is getting near," intertwined with the chant "the whole world's watching" which was recorded live at the infamous 1968 Democratic convention where yippies led by Abby Hoffman, Tom Hayden, Jerry Ruben and other members of the notorious Chicago 7 demonstrated. The album closed on a more hopeful political note with *Liberation*, a 15:41 live instrumental jam session.

CHICAGO TRANSIT AUTHORITY debuted at Number 163 on May 17, 1969. After just one week, the album rocketed to Number 42, peaking at Number 17 by July 19. *Down Beat* magazine stated in their October 2, 1969, issue, "There's 77:43 of music on these two records. 70:50 of it is at least good, and some is very heavy indeed."

But some looked at Chicago Transit Authority as jumping on the brass bus being driven by Blood, Sweat & Tears. The history books will forever compare Blood Sweat &Tears and Chicago, despite their numerous differences. BS&T was a band fronted first by organist and singer Al Kooper, then by singer David Clayton-Thomas. Chicago was fronted by three lead singers, all of whom played instruments and shared the spotlight. BS&T recorded numerous compositions by writers other than those in the band. For their first fourteen albums, Chicago wrote all their own material, except for a cover of The Spencer Davis Group's *I'm A Man* on their first album and a cover of Rufus' *Street Player*

FEELIN' STRONGER EVERY DAY

on CHICAGO 13. (Oddly enough, both bands covered songs written by Steve Winwood: *Smiling Phases* on the BS&T album, and *I'm A Man* on CTA.) BS&T were "groovy" — in the Austin Powers sense of the word. *Playboy After Dark*, the 'swinger's set' — this was the image of BS&T. Chicago was a younger looking and sounding band, rock shaggy and folk rough despite classical training, embraced by the college crowds, as well as fans of music as diverse as Cream and Richie Havens — and young girls. BS&T looked like jazz musicians; Chicago looked like a rock band. Walter Parazaider's rock 'n' roll band with horns was formed February 15, 1967 and spent almost two years rehearsing, playing, writing, and preparing for the release of its first album; Blood, Sweat & Tears was formed in mid-summer 1967 but reached the recording stage sooner because of bandleader Al Kooper's established record industry connections. "I take pride in that we were the first to try this 'rock 'n' roll band with horns' thing," says Parazaider. "Unfortunately — and when you look back at it, I have to say I'm happy with the timing of the way everything happened — we just happened not to be the first 'rock 'n' roll band with horns' to get out there on record."

Despite these differences in image and regardless of the question of who came first, one might still be tempted to place the two bands in the same musical genre. James Guercio produced both artists, they both had horn sections, and they both played jazz-rock. Right? Wrong. BS&T was indeed a jazz band. Jim Fielder was an outstanding jazz bassist, Bobby Colomby an accomplished jazz drummer, and the horn players all blew fine jazz. But something happens when jazz players play rock and roll — it sounds like jazz! While on their first album BS&T sounded like an innovative jazz-rock band, on their second album, aside from the classical pieces, the songs were borderline musical theater/show tunes, with David Clayton Thomas sounding more like Robert Goulet than Robert Plant. Steve Katz's song *Sometimes In Winter* conjures up images of young people in the '60s wearing suede coats and wondering what it all means. Chicago was a *rock* band with a guitar and with classical horns.

"Everybody thought we were college trained," says Peter Cetera on this subject. "In fact, we weren't. The whole rhythm section wasn't. The only guys that actually were going to college were the horn players, and, I believe, Bobby, the keyboard player, was going for a while privately, but, really, in actual fact, Danny, the drummer, myself, Terry Kath, the guitar player, and Bobby were all street musicians. I think particularly in rock music, it's okay to be college-educated, but by no means does it make you better or worse. I think

CHICAGO I

that sometimes the street player has the edge when it comes to rock music. Sometimes, rock music, the more you know, the less you feel."

Walt Parazaider, who gave up a chair in the Chicago symphony to play rock, says it's Cetera who may have the best education of anybody. "Peter was playing when I was playing at 13," he notes, "and his education came from the smoke-filled bars, and you know what? That's a knowledge that you could never flop down your tuition money to get, because I saw both sides of that coin. That is as valid an education as me having the sheepskin on the wall. There were so many diverse personalities in this group that sometimes I had to wonder why this didn't blow up after about a year's worth of success. But we loved music so much. Peter wrote country tunes on the third album. There was also as much diverse interest in all aspects of music. Jimmy Pankow was a stone cold jazzer who loved The Beatles. Lee Loughnane loved playing big band jazz, but loved rock 'n' roll. The same thing with myself. And then you had people who loved the Jimi Hendrix stuff, like Terry, or just rock 'n' roll stuff, like Danny, and if you think about it, there is everything from blues, classical, the big band sound. It became a meld into the band where any kind of music, as long as it was played well, was valid."

Both bands had their imitators. There was Lighthouse in 1970 who had a hit with their BS&T sounding *One Fine Morning*, Looking Glass, whose smash-hit *Brandy* owed everything to Chicago, including a Terry Kath sound-a-like on lead vocals, and less commercially successful groups like Chase, Ten Wheel Drive, Flock, and Cold Blood. Of course, you could argue that R&B and funk legends Earth, Wind & Fire and Tower of Power were also branches on the BS&T/Chicago family tree, and you would have a valid argument.

Oddly enough, the James Guercio produced second BS&T's album barely shipped 5,000 copies. It wasn't until the end of 1969 that the album would become a huge hit, ending up as one of the five biggest selling albums of the year and winning a Grammy for Album of the Year at the February 1970 ceremonies, the same month Chicago released their second album. Ultimately, Blood, Sweat & Tears became history, while Chicago would continue making history.

CHICAGO II

COLUMBIA KGP 24 (S)

Robert Lamm (keyboards and vocals) ⚡ Peter Cetera (bass and vocals) ⚡ Terry Kath (guitar and vocals) ⚡ Danny Seraphine (drums) ⚡ Walter Parazaider (woodwinds) ⚡ James Pankow (trombone) ⚡ Lee Loughnane (trumpet)

Side 1
Moving In
The Road
Poem for the People
In The Country
Side 2
Wake Up Sunshine
(Ballet for a Girl in Buchannon)
1. Make Me Smile
2. So Much to Say; So Much to Give
3. Anxiety's Moment
4. West Virginia Fantasies
5. Colour My World
6. To Be Free
7. Now More Than Ever
Side 3
Fancy Colours
25 Or 6 To 4
Prelude
1. AM Mourning
2. PM Mourning
Memories of Love
Side 4
It Better End Soon
Where Do We Go From Here?

With the release of Chicago's second album, the famous Chicago logo was born. Designed by John Berg and Nick Fasciano, it was part Coca-Cola and part comic book icon. That logo would ultimately be more identifiable than any one person in the band. CHICAGO II, as it was called, was also the official start to the numbering system, as Peter Cetera explains. "People always asked why we were numbering our albums, and the reason is, because we always argued about what to call it. 'All right, III, all right, IV!'"

CHICAGO II was recorded in August 1969, just a mere seven months after the first. The album, also a two-record set, entered the Billboard album chart on February 14, 1970 at Number 44, a far cry from CTA's entrance at Number 163. At that time, LED ZEPPELIN II and The Beatles ABBEY ROAD held the highest chart positions, followed by Credence Clearwater Revival, Tom Jones, The

CHICAGO II

Rolling Stones, and Three-Dog Night. By March 7, 1970, less than one month later, CHICAGO II had shot up to Number 5, surpassing The Jackson 5, Santana, and Three Dog Night. Meanwhile, CTA was still on the charts at Number 44.

CHICAGO II was also well-received critically as a "theme LP set" in the February 17, 1970 issue of *Billboard* magazine: "The sound is big band, with the exception of some interesting progressive rock passages and a rock beat, but the lyrics are strongly in the vein of message tunes of today. 'Make Me Smile' is one of the better cuts . . . 'It Better End Soon' is a good cut, as is 'Fancy Colours.'"

The album yielded some of the band's most memorable songs, including three that would become classics: Robert Lamm's *25 Or 6 To 4* and James Pankow's *Make Me Smile* and *Colour My World*. All three songs would become hits when released as singles. Prior to these songs, AM radio was not very receptive to the band's music. *Beginnings* and *Questions 67 & 68* from CTA were radio tested, but never got off the ground. As Pankow recalls, "I was driving my car down Santa Monica Boulevard in L.A. and I turned the radio on, KHJ, and *Make Me Smile* came on. I almost hit the car in front of me, 'cause it's my song, and I am hearing it on the biggest station in L.A. At that point, I realized, hey, we have a hit single. They don't play you in L.A. unless you're hit-bound. That was one of the more exciting moments in my early career."

> Children play in the park
> They don't know I'm alone in the dark
> Even though time and again I see your face
> Smiling inside
>
> Oh my darling
> Got to have you
> Feel the magic
> When I hold you
> Tell me you will stay
> Make me smile
> — James Pankow, *Make Me Smile* (ASCAP)

Make Me Smile was a Top 10 hit and the album's second single, *25 Or 6 To 4*, reached Number 4 in the summer of 1970. *25 Or 6 To 4*, a song Lamm insists was not about drugs, also did much to associate Peter Cetera's soaring

33

FEELIN' STRONGER EVERY DAY

tenor voice with Chicago. Pop music, throughout its brief history, has seemed to attract tenor vocalists. Fortunately for Chicago, they had the entire spectrum covered with Lamm, Kath, and Cetera.

> Waiting for the break of day
> Searching for something to say
> Flashing lights against the sky
> Giving up I close my eyes
> Sitting cross-legged on the floor
> 25 or 6 to 4
> — Robert Lamm, *25 Or 6 To 4* (ASCAP)

CHICAGO II was not only more popular but also much more musical than CHICAGO TRANSIT AUTHORITY. Songs like *The Road, Movin' In,* and *Wake Up Sunshine* showed a definite maturity in the writing, which was fascinating since the record was made only seven months after the first. *Ballet for a Girl in Buchannon,* or 'The Ballet', as it has come to be known, seemed to be Chicago's version of The Beatles 'A Day in the Life' opus. Just as Kath's *Introduction* from CTA consisted of several emotional movements, 'The 'Ballet' took the listener on a journey across the musical spectrum, from rock to through pop to classical, as the band worked through their own rich musical heritage. *Colour My World,* Chicago's first true ballad, contained a heartfelt vocal performance by Terry Kath and a lilting flute solo by Walter Parazaider. James Pankow has stated that Frank Sinatra once asked the band to write a second verse so that he might cover the song. Pankow respectfully declined.

> As time goes on I realize
> Just what you mean to me
> And now, now that you're near
> Promise your love that I've waited to share
> And dreams of our moments together
> Colour my world with hope
> Of loving you
> — James Pankow, *Colour My World* (ASCAP)

CHICAGO II also delved deeper into the political arena that was touched on in the first record. *It Better End Soon,* a plea to end the Vietnam War

CHICAGO II

with lyrics that urged people to be responsible in their fight against 'the system', written by Lamm, Parazaider, and Kath, is an in-your-face, extended track with solos and a 'sermon' by Terry Kath.

> Can't stand it no more The people dying crying for help for so many years But nobody hears Better end soon my friend It better end soon my friend . . . Hey, everybody Won't you just look around Can't anybody see? Just what's going down . . . They're killing everybody I wish it weren't true They say we got to make war Or the economy will fail But if we don't stop We won't be around no more . . .
> — Robert Lamm/Terry Kath, *It Better End Soon* (ASCAP)

The liner notes contained the complete lyrics to *It Better End Soon* as well as a statement signed by the whole band "dedicating ourselves, our futures and our energies to the people of the revolution — And the revolution in all its forms."

Peter Cetera's *Where Do We Go From Here* could also be taken as a political commentary. "I had just gotten out of the hospital," Cetera recalls, "and was lying in my bed, convalescing, when they landed on the moon, and I grabbed my bass guitar and started this little progression on bass, and started writing, *Where Do We Go From Here*. I think Walter Kronkite actually had said that, and I thought, 'Wow, where do we go from here?' So, in a melancholy way, I wrote it about that, and then I wrote it out myself, about the world, and about everything in general, and that was my first writing credit."

> Every day just gets a little shorter, don't you think?
> Take a look around and you'll see just what I mean
> People got to come together not just out of fear
> Where do we go . . . Where do we go . . . Where do we go from here?
> — Peter Cetera, *Where Do We Go From Here* (ASCAP)

One place Chicago did go was on the road, touring in support of the album. The band had already been on the road virtually non-stop since February 1969, closing that year with their first European tour. According to the information provided in the LIVE AT CARNEGIE HALL (CHICAGO IV) collection, Chicago played 161 dates in 1970 across the United States. Many of these dates were at universities, colleges, and even some high schools. Chicago was reaching a highly important demographic group — the college crowd.

FEELIN' STRONGER EVERY DAY

If the college crowd deemed you cool, you were cool. After the success of *Make Me Smile* and *25 Or 6 To 4*, CBS and Chicago did something clever and unusual; they went back to the first album for the next single. Robert Lamm's *Does Anybody Really Know What Time It Is?* — one of the more jazz-influenced songs — became the third hit single, reaching the Top 10 by the beginning of 1971.

1971 saw Chicago mount a full-scale world tour with stops in England, Germany, Italy, France, and Japan. Once again, playing well over 150 dates, often ten to twelve days straight with no break. It's no secret why this band became so big so fast. Two simple words: hard work. One of the people who helped make these tours successful was Bob Ludwig, a native of San Bernardino who studied in electronics school for two years before beginning his long career as one of the top live sound engineers in the music business. A guitarist and music buff, Ludwig never imagined himself becoming involved in the entertainment industry. "Out of default," he says, "I ended up in the entertainment industry 'cause there wasn't any other work around, and immediately found myself relocated to Hollywood, where I started working on equipment — this was around 1969 — for various groups like Three Dog Night, Steppenwolf, The Beach Boys, and, later, Chicago."

The company that employed Bob was called Solid Sound. Operating out of the back of a music store owned by Randy Carlton, a partner in Solid Sound, Ludwig began forming relationships with the music community. "We had a company in the back [of the Music Center], and that's where all the groups would come in," he explains. "So I would meet the groups as they would come in for musical instruments, and then we'd take them in the back and sell them on our sound services. We were also building equipment back then, and with my background, I was building and designing power amps and mixing consoles. In those days, you didn't just walk in and buy a PM 1000 mixing console. They didn't exist. Everything was custom made — almost everything." Ludwig and company wound up building high-class consoles from scratch.

Bob Ludwig's first experience mixing live sound with his custom made boards was with The Beach Boys. "The Beach Boys was one of the first tours I went on," says Ludwig." The stuff I did [with them] was all in California. I had never really went on the road, around the country." His lengthy road experience was about to start with the building of equipment for Chicago. "I was asked to build a new mixing console for Chicago," he remembers. "Apparently, we had come in contact with them. So I built them a new 24-channel console for their tour, which, in 1970, was a pretty elaborate piece of equipment. Prior to that, they were using an old P.A.; it might have been a Sunn mixing console, with some old speaker boxes. We wanted to upgrade them into the '70s!"

Bob recalls getting the order to go out and do sound on the road for the band, which came with the request to build the new equipment. "One of the other owners of Solid Sound was a guy by the name of William 'Skip' Bennett. Skip had a lot of road experience where Randy didn't. Skip had been on the road with Three Dog Night for a number of years. He was their equipment guy. He knew the equipment, he knew sound, and he knew how the stuff was to be put together." Bob points out that sound equipment, at that time, was "in a state of evolution," and that Solid Sound was in the development of a lot of the systems and products that ended up on tours later on. "Skip, with his knowledge," he continues, "was involved with the company, so he immediately jumped on the Chicago issue to put together a P.A. system we could take out on the road and start doing shows [with Chicago]." While it was Skip Bennett who initially worked the new console for Chicago, it was time for Ludwig to take the reins. "I can't remember exactly how long [Skip] had been out there, but it was time for me to kinda join up with them. I kinda had the itch to get out of the shop and get on the road, because I was young and I wanted to see the country."

His first encounter with Chicago was in Knoxville, Tennessee. "I'd never seen Chicago before," he confesses. "As a matter of fact, when I learned I was gonna go do this, I'd never even really listened to Chicago! I knew who they were, but I never bothered to really sit down and listen." In his defense, this was 1970 and the band had only two albums out at the time, so it wasn't like he was ignorant to a huge body of work. "About a month before I went to do this," he backtracks, " I had a chance to go up to Canada with a friend of mine, in a little VW, and I said, 'Hey, Vinnie, I'm gonna go do Chicago in a month,' and he went, 'Wow! That's great!' It just so happens that he had all their albums, and I think they only had two at the time, and I listened from beginning to end, and I just sat there in awe and went 'That's incredible! (Laughing) I'm gonna work with these guys? That's the best stuff I ever heard!' I was knocked out." He also remembers the radio stations playing a lot of Chicago, especially *I'm A Man*, all the way up to Canada. "By the time I got to Knoxville, I was all primed to see the band. Now, I've heard their music, and, to me, to this day, that was some of the best music I think they've ever done — from a musical

FEELIN' STRONGER EVERY DAY

point of view. Maybe it didn't sell a lot of records for them, but to me, it was beyond genius." He added that he felt the band's first three albums were "way beyond their time."

Admittedly, Bob doesn't have much memory of the first show he did with Chicago. "I just remember sitting there, watching the show, and I was kinda just in awe, because it was the first time I'd ever been on the road, the first time I'd ever seen Chicago, and I was, like, 'Wow — pinch me! Is this real?' (Laughs) After packing the gear, Ludwig and the band hit the road. "In those days," he says, "we did one-nighters, and the band was used to doing, like, 28 shows every month, year round." He brings up the fact that Chicago listed all these gigs in the copious liner notes from LIVE AT CARNEGIE HALL. "It would be 300 shows, plus, per year," he emphasizes.

Bob recounts one particularly eventful show at Georgia's Lake Spivey. "Some promoter had put together this show out on a peninsula on Lake Spivey, and the stage is right on the tip of the peninsula. We set up, it's Georgia, it's real green, it's like a park, but back in those days, in 1970-1971, rednecks and longhairs were a big issue." He remembers how nerve wracking it was driving through parts of the country with three trucks filled with equipment and rock and rollers. "We set up, we did the sound check, and we're ready for the show. The band comes out, the stage lights come up, it's just after dark, but it's summer time, so there's still kinda twilight. We do just like a half of a song and all the power goes out. Turns out that someone drove by out on the highway and put a bullet through the transformer and it shorted out all the power!" With no power, and no way to communicate with the crowd, he remembers the scene turning ugly. "We've got probably ten-thousand people out on this peninsula, with us at the very end, and no way to get out of there. These people were rather patient for the first couple of hours! We're sitting out there, it's completely dark, there's no way to talk to [the crowd], and it starts to get rowdy. Cans and stuff start hitting the stage, rocks are hitting the stage. Finally, we get a little generator, and we plug in one amp and one speaker with a microphone, so we can talk with the people and calm them down a little bit. Finally, about twelve or one-o-clock in the morning, the Edison Company shows up with a new transformer. They have to make their way through the crowd, they put it right next to the stage, and they take these sticks and go up to the telephone pole and hook it right onto a high voltage [line]. We hooked in our power, it took us a few minutes to hook all that up, and we get up and running, and it's Show Time."

CHICAGO II

Bob recalls that, after all the down time, the band had become "sauced. These guys were just ripped!" Nevertheless, the band played a great show. "I tell ya, they started playing and it was like magic. This band just came alive, and the people just went nuts. It was such a special show because of what we had to go through to get the show on." After packing up in the wee hours of the morning, Bob had his first encounter with groupies. "Girls are coming up and hanging on and stuff, and I was, like, 'Wow! I've never seen this before!' (Laughs) That was great!"

The band then headed for Birmingham, Alabama, where, Bob says, "the only thing eventful was driving through Alabama late at night and stopping for gas. We had to run to the trucks and split before the rednecks came out! They were all looking at us — we couldn't wait to get out of the South!" Bob is reminded of another Chicago gig in Birmingham, Alabama some years later, where a young man by the name of Bruce Springsteen opened the show. "This guy was from the East Coast," says Bob, "and nobody had ever heard of him. He had a couple of albums out but they were awful compared to the way he sounded live. The producer had failed to capture the energy of this guy's live show. I remember telling a friend, 'Hey, this guy is gonna be the next Bob Dylan!" Ludwig actually had an audiotape of the Springsteen/Chicago shows, but, unfortunately, his house was destroyed by fire in 1978. That tape, along with many other precious mementos and memorabilia are gone forever.

Despite the exhaustive, jaw-dropping tour schedule, Chicago found time to record their third double album entitled, yes, folks, CHICAGO III.

CHICAGO III

COLUMBIA C2 30110 (S)

Peter Cetera (bass, steel guitar, vocals) ∿ Terry Kath (guitar and vocals) ∿ Robert Lamm (keyboards and vocals) ∿ Lee Loughnane (trumpet) ∿ James Pankow (trombone) ∿ Walter Parazaider (woodwinds) ∿ Daniel Seraphine (drums and timbales)

Side 1
Sing A Mean Tune Kid
Loneliness Is Just A Word
What Else Can I Say
I Don't Want Your Money

Side 2
Travel Suite:
Flight 602
Motorboat To Mars
Free
Free Country
At The Sunrise
Happy 'Cause I'm Going Home

Side 3
Mother
Lowdown
An Hour In The Shower
A Hard Risin' Morning
 Without Breakfast
Off To Work
Fallin' Out
Dreamin' Home
Morning Blues Again

Side 4
Elegy:
When All The Laughter
 Dies In Sorrow
Canon
Once Upon A Time . . .
Progress
The Approaching Storm
Man Vs. Man = The End

S porting a pseudo-revolutionary flag flying the band's logo, CHICAGO III was released in January 1971 and entered the *Billboard* charts at Number 22, their highest debut to date. Even more impressive was the fact that CHICAGO II was holding at Number 16 and CTA was still going strong at Number 49. The new album received a warm welcome from the critics at *Billboard* magazine: "Chicago and its horns of plenty offer its 3rd double LP in as many releases and once again quality exceeds quantity. 'Loneliness Is Just A Word,' 'What Else Can I Say,' and 'Free' (from side 2's Travel Suite) are the most commercial vocals, while two instrumentals from side 4's Elegy, 'Progress' with its man made sound effects and the jazzy 'The Approaching Storm,' should

CHICAGO III

be popular cuts." By February 20, 1971, CHICAGO III had peaked at Number 2, sandwiched between the JESUS CHRIST SUPER STAR soundtrack and George Harrison's ALL THINGS MUST PASS.

Very impressive, for a double album which was done on the fly. According to what Walter Parzaider told William James Ruhlman, author of the liner notes to Chicago's group portrait boxed set, released in 1991 by Columbia/Legacy, "We basically had run out of the surplus (of songs) that we had, and we were still working a lot on the road. I think we were a little afraid that we were writing and rehearsing and getting ready to record a little under the gun." Parazaider also credits James William Guercio for "coordinating all this stuff and keeping us inspired. A hell of a producer."

One would have to agree with Parazaider, who also stated that despite whatever fear and anxiety the writers and the musicians may have felt, "I don't think it shows on that album, I think what came out of there was some strong stuff."

Although CHICAGO III was a major success, the singles pulled form the album did not fare too well. The first, Robert Lamm's *Free*, a powerful anthem for the oppressed, failed to break out of the Top 20. The second single, *Lowdown*, written by Peter Cetera and drummer Danny Seraphine, was even more lackluster, never rising above the 'Bottom 40'. Cetera does not have fond memories of his second offering as a writer. "I was very proud of it, but one thing bad is that Terry said, 'Don't you ever tell anybody I played guitar on this record,' and he proceeded to play the song exactly like that, and that leaves a bad taste in my mouth. Terry kind of played that song with an I-don't-give-a-shit attitude, and actually when he did that to that song, it in effect kind of took any heart out of it. I was never really happy with the outcome 'cause it was played with one or two takes in mind. I'm still proud of it, it's one of the first things I did, and every person has to have a start."

Relying on what worked before, Columbia reached back to the first and second albums for singles and came up with *Beginnings* and *Colour My World* on one '45 which hit Number 7 by August. The following month *Questions 67 & 68*, now two years old, was released and became a Top 30 hit. *Cashbox* magazine charted it at Number 13.

CHICAGO III also showed substantial growth on behalf of the writers. Robert Lamm's *Mother* was an ambitious piece about the destruction of the environment, complete with an interestingly dissonant horn arrangement led by James Pankow's trombone.

FEELIN' STRONGER EVERY DAY

> Driving down the concrete beams
> Looking around and now it seems
> Mama Earth is nowhere
> Gone from your eyes
> Hidden in the crust
> Of man's scientific dreams
> She is gone
> — Robert Lamm, *Mother* (ASCAP)

Loneliness Is Just a Word, also penned by Lamm, continued in the jazz-rock tradition. Vocal harmonies were in top-notch form throughout the double disc set. Songs like Lamm's *At the Sunrise* and *Happy 'Cause I'm Going Home*, as well as *Dreamin' Home/Morning Blues Again*, both part of Terry Kath's *An Hour In The Shower*, showed just how awesome the Chicago vocal power could be. Aside from Cetera and Seraphine's internally controversial *Lowdown*, Cetera provided another tune, *What Else Can I Say*. Decidedly Beatle-esque, this tune also featured Cetera on pedal steel guitar, which was also present on Lamm's *Flight 602*, part of his "Travel Suite."

In retrospect, CHICAGO III may have been the best of the band's early work. All the touring and writing made the band tight and unified, and there was a perfect blend of group identity and individual diversity present on this album, more so than the previous endeavors. Many fans took CHICAGO III as the point at which to stop listening to the band, feeling that it marked the end of their best work. Others were not taken with the band until the subsequent albums. Either way, two things were certain — if Chicago had never recorded again, the body of work they had created with CTA, II, and III would have guaranteed them a place in music history, for quality if not for quantity, to paraphrase the *Billboard* review of CHICAGO III.

CHICAGO III

Publicity photo for CHICAGO TRANSIT AUTHORITY album release, circa 1969.

Portraits of Chicago from
CHICAGO II, circa 1970.

James Pankow

Walt Parazaider

Lee Loughnane

CHICAGO III

Danny Seraphine

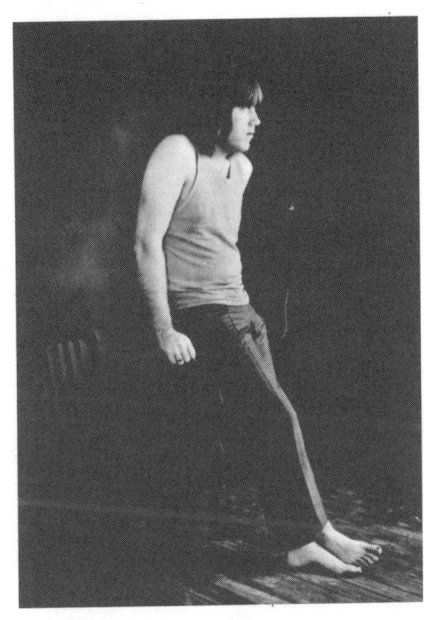

Terry Kath

Peter Cetera

Robert Lamm

FEELIN' STRONGER EVERY DAY

DePaul University School of Music (top), display of Chicago memorabilia at Demon Dogs restaurant in Chicago (middle), and plaque for the Terry Kath Memorial Scholarship at DePaul.

CHICAGO III

Backstage pass from the second Chicago/Beach Boys tour (top left), advertisement from TV GUIDE for a Chicago television special (top right), and Chicago concert poster (bottom).

FEELIN' STRONGER EVERY DAY

CHICAGO III

Live at Nassau Coliseum, 1977.

FEELIN' STRONGER EVERY DAY

Terry Kath, circa 1969.

CHICAGO IV

LIVE AT CARNEGIE HALL

COLUMBIA C4X30865

Robert Lamm (keyboards and vocals) ∞ Peter Cetera (bass and vocals) ∞ Terry Kath (guitar and vocals) ∞ Daniel Seraphine (drums) ∞ Lee Loughnane (guitar, percussion, trumpet, background vocals) ∞ James Pankow (percussion and trombone) ∞ Walter Parazaider (woodwinds, percussion, background vocals)

Side 1
In the Country
Fancy Colours
Does Anybody Really Know What Time It Is?
(Free Form Intro)
Does Anybody Really Know What Time It Is?

Side 2
South California Purples
Questions 67 and 68

Side 3
Sing A Mean Tune Kid
Beginnings

Side 4
It Better End Soon - 1st Movement
It Better End Soon - 2nd Movement
(Flute Solo)
It Better End Soon - 3rd Movement
(Guitar Solo)
It Better End Soon - 4th Movement
(Preach)
It Better End Soon - 5th Movement

Side 5
Introduction
Mother
Lowdown

Side 6
Flight 602
Motorboat to Mars
Free
Where Do We Go From Here
I Don't Want Your Money

Side 7
Happy 'Cause I'm Going Home
Ballet For a Girl In Buchannon
Make Me Smile
So Much To Say, So Much To Give
West Virginia Fantasies
Colour My World
To Be Free
Now More Than Ever

Side 8
A Song For Richard And His Friends
25 Or 6 To 4
I'm A Man

FEELIN' STRONGER EVERY DAY

Chicago's next album, LIVE AT CARNEGIE HALL, would become their most infamous work and the trial by fire that created a whole new Chicago. From April 5 through 10, 1971, Chicago played at New York's Carnegie Hall, and James Guercio decided to record the band live. Released as a four record boxed set, the album was a fan's dreams come true, at least in terms of packaging. One of the biggest color posters ever to grace a Chicago fan's wall was inserted in the box. Designed by Ron Coro, it measured six-feet wide and four-feet long and featured a collage of photos of the band taken from the performances by Fred Lombardi. The package also included a picture book and a chronology of every live gig the band played from May of 1967 to November of 1971.

It was that extravagant packaging that caused Guercio to clash with Clive Davis and CBS. "I had a big fight with Clive over the package," says Guercio. "They thought I was extravagant. I said, 'What is this all about? A dollar nineteen? Eighty-nine cents? Listen, I'm paying for it. What do you mean? I said, 'I will pay. What's your break-even? What's your break point?' 'Well, if we sell 500,000, the cost of the package goes down dramatically.' And that was the agreement I made on that record, I remember very well. I said, 'If it doesn't sell a million units, send me the bill. Now shut up! What's next?' That's how the package happened. I rolled the dice everytime 'cause I believed in what I was doing."

But the critics shot the Carnegie Hall album to pieces — and so did the band. The word-of-mouth was that Chicago was a great studio band but couldn't cut it live. As Peter Cetera stated in the liner notes from the 1991 CD box set, "The Carnegie Hall Album was one of the things that started out to be a plus, but ended up being a big minus."

Over the years, Chicago had not been without detractors. In *Rolling Stone* magazine, on March 18, 1971, Lester Bangs fired off the kind of review which became more common as Chicago became more popular and played more pop-oriented music in the 1970s. "Up until now, bands like B,S&T and Chicago have been ponderous in a way that is inimical to both rock and jazz," Bangs wrote. "With Ellington or Basie, for instance, whole brass sections could swing with the grace and fluidity of a single soloist, but few of our pop melanges have that much tightness or discipline, so they settle for the brute force of numbers and volume, and a spurious versatility which heaps styles, solos and arrangements raided from the whole range of venerable rock, jazz and classical sources.

CHICAGO IV

"Another problem is that the overkill arrangements and numbers of musicians involved in these projects tend to take the heat off individual writers and soloists. The results amount to a wholesale substitution of quantity for quality. Compositions are seldom real songs, but rather imitations of songs, with lyrics stapled onto arrangements fitted for large ensembles. Solos are seldom real solos but rather long strings of solos that taken separately (or placed in a humbler context) would amount to nothing more than some obviously inferior cabaret work.

"Chicago has been a prime perpetrator of all these offenses. Every release a double album, they lack truly outstanding soloists, and the stiffness of such songs as *25 Or 6 To 4* is as far from the spirit of rock and jazz as the long pretentious suites that the group has thus far found irresistible. Happily, CHICAGO III, while it contains all the weaknesses that have dragged them down in the past, is the best thing they have done and succeeds as pure entertainment by de-emphasizing the long solos and concentrating on solidly conceived tunes and gimmicks, which while they smack of Hollywood, are fun to listen to at that very level. Another plus is the marked improvement in the instrumental work. The ensembles are generally tight and clean, and except for lapses in taste on the part of the otherwise talented guitarist, Terry Kath, the solos are quite impressive.

"Still, on CHICAGO III the group excels most as collectors of a whole range of styles. In the course of the four sides, they take us through another of those waltz-like things with a neo-jazz vocal (*Loneliness Is Just A Word*) to the Springfield-CSN&Y bag (*Flight 602*) and then mold the latter with Abbey Road riffs into one dynamite single (*What Else Can I Say*). Whether or not they ever find a style their own is questionable, but then this is probably not their function, anyway."

In an interview with *Down Beat* magazine, Peter Cetera responded with his own irreverent opinion of *Rolling Stone*. "You know, as far as *Rolling Stone* goes," says Cetera. "I read it all the time, mostly when I'm taking a shit. I always buy it and they have given us seven bad reviews on seven straight albums and every one's sold a million. It's probably that somewhere along the line we didn't kiss ass and it really pissed off some guy in the front office. It's come to the point that now I really enjoy waiting for a *Rolling Stone* review of our album so I can see what they're going to say bad about it."

The main criticism of the Carnegie Hall album was not as well reasoned as Lester Bang's opinion; rather, the negative comments were directed

FEELIN' STRONGER EVERY DAY

towards the 'live' quality of the production.

Robert Lamm, however, defends the album as an accurate record of what happened. "I have rarely ever heard a live recording that wasn't studio-enhanced later on that really sounded anything like a studio recording," he notes. "But what this was supposed to capture was an event and the excitement and the things that happened when a band plays live, and I think it does that famously. That was an exciting week, to actually play in Carnegie Hall."

Concert sound in 1971, even state-of-the-art, was not as highly evolved as the music it was conveying — and Carnegie Hall was not exactly the ideal venue for Chicago's massive sound, as Bob Ludwig, who was mixing sound during Chicago's week at Carnegie Hall, notes. "I don't really remember any of the problems other than the fact that it was Carnegie Hall," he says, "and that, acoustically, it was not a great place for a rock concert." He does remember, however, that the New York unions clashed with the Chicago crew, probably a home-town rivalry. "They were yelling at us, 'You'll never play here again!' and we yelled back, 'That's fine 'cause we're not coming back!'" Add to all of these technical problems the report that producer James Guercio had accused the band of being drunk and sloppy, and you have the makings of a sorely hampered performance

Released in October of 1971, CHICAGO LIVE AT CARNEGIE HALL, despite the slings and arrows, was a hit. Shipping gold and entering the Billboard Album Chart at Number 43 in November 1971, it quickly became one of the best-selling boxed sets by a rock group ever. With CARNEGIE HALL in the Top 40, CTA was sitting at Number 37 after 131 weeks on the charts, while its partners, CHICAGO II and III, were at Number 88 and 90, respectively.

Despite being touted by Guercio and CBS as the Rolls Royce of Rock, the class act with the classical numbering system and the bone white, silhouetted package of the four disc set, Chicago did not become complacent, the criticisms serving to stir them to improve their performance and productions. Chicago's next endeavor would prove to be their most successful, well-crafted record to date.

CHICAGO V

COLUMBIA KG 31102

Terry Kath (guitar and vocals) ∞ Peter Cetera (bass and vocals) ∞ Robert Lamm (keyboards and vocals) ∞ Lee Loughnane (trumpet, background vocals, percussion) ∞ Walter Parazaider (woodwinds, percussion) ∞ James Pankow (trombone, percussion) ∞ Danny Seraphine (antique bells, congas, drums)

Side 1	Side 2
A Hit by Varese	While the City Sleeps
All Is Well	Saturday in the Park
Now That You've Gone	State of the Union
Dialogue	Goodbye
(Part One)	Alma Mater
(Part Two)	

CHICAGO V, released in July 1972, debuted in *Billboard* at Number 39. By August 19, 1972, the album went all the way to Number 1. Chicago had become one of the most popular bands in America, soaring past legendary artists like Elton John, The Rolling Stones, and Simon & Garfunkel.

Recorded in just eight days in September 1971, CHICAGO V was a musical milestone on many levels. First, it was the band's first single disc record. Second, the songs were more streamlined than ever. Gone were all the lengthy instrumental jams and avant-garde neo-classical explorations. CHICAGO V showed a dignified restraint that took their music to a new level. Robert Lamm's *A Hit By Varese* and *Goodbye* were every bit as dynamic and thoughtful as his earlier work, showcasing everything that set this group apart from its pretenders and contemporaries — Terry Kath's outstanding guitar work, the brilliant horn arrangements, and the impeccable vocals. Another track, *Dialogue*, which is split into Part I and Part II, is a musical conversation between Terry Kath and Peter Cetera, featuring Cetera's best bass playing ever. The rhythm section is so incredibly musical during Part I that it would stand alone as its own performance. As with CHICAGO III, the vocal harmonies continued to shine, especially on Lamm's *All is Well* and *Dialogue*, Part II. Terry Kath's *Alma Mater* also provided a perfect landscape for the vocalists.

Billboard gave the album a rave review on November 6, 1972: "The long-awaited new LP from Chicago was well worth waiting for. The super heavy package contains some nine new numbers that will prove strong programmers. Highlight cuts include 'Saturday in the Park,' 'While the City Sleeps,' 'All Is Well,' and an interesting reflection on politics, 'Dialogue.' Their first single record will prove a giant."

Robert Lamm was exceptionally proficient on this album, writing eight of the ten songs. *Goodbye*, a beautifully haunting introspective/retrospective account of the band's career, and perhaps Lamm's own life, sung by Peter Cetera, keeps alive the jazz-rock spirit without being camp.

> Flying high, touch the sky
> Going to places I never knew
> So Goodbye
> And hello, long ago
>
> I can see history
> Standing still, a mystery
> If you will, pardon me
> I'm away for the day
> Feels so good to be soaring
> 'Cause L.A. was so boring
> Goodbye
>
> There must be room for growing
> Somewhere else and I'm going
> Goodbye
>
> — Robert Lamm, Goodbye (ASCAP)

CHICAGO V contained one single song written by Lamm that would introduce the band to an entirely new audience and prove to be a harbinger of things to come. *Saturday in the Park* was a radical departure for the band. While Lamm and Cetera had exhibited an ability to write pop songs earlier on with CHICAGO II's *Where Do We Go From Here* and III's *At the Sunrise, What Else Can I Say*, and *Lowdown*, nothing compared to the commercial accessibility of *Saturday In the Park*. It seemed somewhat out of place when listened

CHICAGO V

to in conjunction with the rest of CHICAGO V, but when you consider that Chicago didn't quite follow any rules or formats, it was right at home. *Saturday in the Park* hit the *Billboard* singles chart at Number 40 and peaked at Number 3. The album held on to the Number 1 spot for two months until the SUPERFLY soundtrack dethroned it on October 21, 1972.

> Saturday in the park, I think it was the Fourth of July
> Saturday in the park, I think it was the Fourth of July
> People dancing, people laughing
> A man selling ice cream, singing Italian songs . . .
> — Robert Lamm, Saturday in the Park (ASCAP)

The audience who would respond positively to *Saturday in the Park* would not necessarily embrace Chicago's existing body of work. (And vice versa.) But when you listen closely to the tune, there's a level of musicianship present that was a cut above most of the hit pop records being made at the time. Peter Cetera and Danny Seraphine provided a funky, almost R&B, foundation for Lamm and Kath to compose and chord over. In fact, Terry Kath's rhythm guitar part is very reminiscent of some of the Motown singles by The Four Tops and The Temptations. With the tremendous success of *Saturday in the Park*, Chicago was on their way to becoming bona-fide superstars. But not individually. . . .

From the start, Chicago was a band that took a conceptual approach to the way it was presented to the public, and that approach was the brainchild of manager/producer Jim Guercio. "I invented the logo," he notes. "The guy that designed it was Nick Fasciano. John Berg was the head of the art department." The Chicago logo has adorned every album cover in the catalog. "Guercio was insistent upon the logo being the dominant factor in the artwork," says James Pankow, "but he was also interested in maintaining a variety approach to the logo on every album." But the logo seemed to overwhelm the identity of individual band members. With five hit albums and a gold single to their name, the band members still remained nameless and faceless to the average listener. Remember this was a decade before music videos and MTV. There was still an air of romantic mystery surrounding rock music and musicians. Mick Jagger, Keith Richards, John, Paul, Ringo, and George were all stars with and without their bands. Eric Clapton, Jimmy Page, and Robert Plant were always in the news, always in the spotlight. You could pick up most rock magazines during the 1970s and read about any one of these people and/or their bands . . . but not

FEELIN' STRONGER EVERY DAY

Chicago. If this band was having any sort of crisis, it was well hidden. You rarely, if ever, heard about anybody in the group from the media. To most, Chicago was the logo, the music, the blond-haired guy with the high voice, the guy with the rough voice, the guy who sings *Saturday in the Park*, and the rest of those guys.

While CHICAGO V and *Saturday In The Park* ruled the charts and the airwaves, James William Guercio was making a movie, *Electra Glide in Blue*. The film starred Robert Blake as a police officer and featured Terry Kath and Peter Cetera as outlaws. Lee Loughnane and Walter Parazaider also had screen time as mud-dwelling hippies. Cetera had the biggest role, playing a bad guy biker who was involved in a high-speed chase, got thrown off his motorcycle, and roughed up by the cops. Kath appeared at the end of the movie, his character shooting and killing Robert Blake's police officer character. It's basically a story of a policeman on motorcycle duty wishing to make detective. When he finally gets the chance to join the 'elite', he screws up by having an affair with the girlfriend of his boss, who doesn't like it at all. Blake is put back on regular duty. You sense that his dream of being a detective is gone and something tragic has to happen to him. It happens to him when he stops a hippie (Terry Kath) for a minor traffic violation and forgets to give the hippie his license back and then tries to flag the hippie down when he follows after him. Guercio employed several members of Chicago to perform on the film's soundtrack, which sounded very much like a Chicago record. *Electra Glide in Blue* has since garnered something of a cult status over the years.

The next single pulled from CHICAGO V was *Dialogue* (Part 1 & 2), which had been edited down from it's original 7:09 to a radio-friendly 4:53. The song peaked at Number 24 in *Billboard*, but reached Number 17 in *Cashbox*, which reported sales only. The song's political content and reference to keeping a "steady high" may have been too much for radio.

Terry
Are you optimistic
'bout the way things are going?

Peter
No, I never ever think of it at all

CHICAGO V

Terry
Don't you ever worry
When you see what's going down?

Peter
No, I try to mind my business
That is, no business at all

Terry
When it's time to function
As a feeling human being, will your
Bachelor of Arts help you get by?

Peter
I hope to study further
A few more years or so
I also hope to keep a steady high...
— Robert Lamm, *Dialogue, Part I* (ASCAP)

CHICAGO V would be the last album to be totally recorded in New York. From this point on, a new sound and a new Chicago would be born.

In February 1972, Chicago mounted its first full-scale world tour during which the band recorded a second, far superior, live album in Japan in June 1972 at the Osaka Festival Hall. "The Japanese had us all wired up for sound, and it was not obvious, there was nothing there," recalls Peter Cetera, in contrast to the terribly obvious recording equipment at Carnegie Hall. The technology was in fact more extensive. "The Japanese hooked up two eight track machines together to make sixteen tracks," notes Parazaider. "The performances were there, and the quality of the sound was really excellent. That's a good live album." The LP was released a few years later only in Japan, but became available as an import in the U.S. in the late '70s. The record features Peter Cetera singing *Questions 67 & 68* and *Lowdown* — in Japanese! Cetera stated in a Los Angeles radio interview in 1984 that this was one of the stranger things he'd ever done. LIVE IN JAPAN also offered a Terry Kath song that would be recorded by the group five years later, on their eleventh album, *Mississippi Delta City Blues*. The double-disc set is

FEELIN' STRONGER EVERY DAY

now available on CD and is part of the Chicago catalog.

Bob Ludwig remembers that tour as well. "We were mobbed!" he says. "When we landed at the airport, there were — I don't know how many — people just screaming 'Chi-ca-go! Chi-ca-go!' And at the hotel, there were crowds of people who stayed out there all day and night with signs, hoping to see the band and get an autograph." The following for Chicago world-wide would only grow with the release of the next album, featuring such classic hits as *Feelin' Stronger Every Day* and *Just You 'N Me*.

CHICAGO VI

COLUMBIA KC 32400

Peter Cetera ∿ Danny Seraphine ∿ Robert Lamm ∿ Lee Loughnane ∿ Walter Parazaider ∿ Terry Kath ∿ James Pankow.

∿

Also featuring guest musicians: Laudir Soares de Oliveira (congas) ∿ Joe Cala (congas) ∿ J.G. O'Rafferty (pedal steel)

Side 1
Critics' Choice
Just You 'N Me
Darlin' Dear
Jenny
What's This World Comin' To

Side 2
Something In This City
Changes People
Hollywood
In Terms of Two
Rediscovery
Feelin' Stronger Every Day

For CHICAGO VI, the band packed their bags and moved into James Guercio's brand new, state-of-the-art recording facility in Nederland, Colorado called Caribou Ranch. In February 1973, Chicago 'christened' the studio by starting their sixth album. "We got a little tired of recording in New York, with maids beating on our hotel room door, with the city bustling around," says Parazaider. "That ended an era, for the time being, and the sixth, seventh, eighth, tenth, and eleventh albums were done up at Caribou Ranch, 8,500 feet up in the Rockies, about an hour's drive outside of Boulder."

Although the ranch was intended to facilitate uninterrupted work, things didn't quite work out that way. "It was nice in a way," Parazaider allows, "but after two or three weeks, our productivity waned. You could go up there and snowmobile if it was winter, you could ride a horse and get away from stuff, you could walk in the woods. He had 3,000 acres up there. But after two or three weeks, I had to go over the wall and go down to the city and just see what the heck was going on. It got so quiet, the silence was deafening. It bothered me. We never did more than two or three weeks at a time after that sixth album." CHICAGO VI has an easy, organic sound. The production and

FEELIN' STRONGER EVERY DAY

the performances gelled better than on the previous records. New York may have provided the perfect environment for Chicago's earlier material to take shape, but the music being made up in the Rockies sounded far more relaxed. It breathed more.

In June 1973, the first results of the Caribou Ranch sessions were released in the form of the future-classic single, *Feelin' Stronger Every Day*. "I can remember the exact beginnings of that one," recalls Peter Cetera, who co-wrote the rock song that returned Chicago to the Top 10. "We were at the Akron Rubber Bowl, in Akron, Ohio, an outdoor gig that was delayed a bit because of rain. And so, we got there our normal hour and a half before the gig, and we're sitting around, and we were told we're gonna hold for at least an hour, and I heard Jimmy Pankow in the other room playing the actual beginning of that song, and I said, 'Well, that's nice.' I walked over, and I said, 'What is that?' and he went, 'Oh, I don't now, I'm just messing around.' So, I said, 'Well, God, I like that,' and he goes, 'You do?' and I went, 'Yeah.' I went and got my bass, and we sat there and played around with it, and a few weeks later, after we got off the road, I went to his house, and we wrote *Feelin' Stronger Every Day*. The song has a lyric with a curious twist on romantic breakup, the narrator declaring himself on the road to recovery rather than dwelling on the split. To Pankow, it also had an implied message for the band. "*Feelin' Stronger Every Day* was about a relationship," he says, "but yet, underlying that relationship it's almost like the band is feeling stronger than ever."

> I do believe in you and I know you believe in me
> Oh yes, oh yes
> But now the time has come for both of us to live on the run
> Oh yes, oh yes
> Knowing that you would have wanted it this way
> I do believe I'm feelin' stronger every day ...
> — Peter Cetera/James Pankow, *Feelin' Stronger Every Day* (ASCAP)

The up-beat *Feelin' Stronger Every Day*, which closes the album, suggests a new direction for the band, while Robert Lamm's *Critics' Choice*, which opens CHICAGO VI, responds to critics like Lester Bangs. Lamm, always a present-tense sort of writer, leads it off with his answer to Chicago's negative reviews, plaintively asking, "What do you want?" before lambasting the critics as parasites in this solo piano/vocal piece.

CHICAGO VI

What do you want?
What do you want?
I'm giving everything I have
I'm even trying to see if there's more
Locked deep inside
I'll try
I'll try
Can't you see this is me?

You parasite
You're dynamite
An oversight
Misunderstanding what you hear
You're quick to jeer
And volunteer
Absurdities, musical blasphemies
Oh Lord
Save us all
— Robert Lamm, *Critics' Choice* (Big Elk Music/ASCAP)

"When I wrote *Critics' Choice*, I was wounded," Lamm explains, "because I always felt like we were coming from an honest place and that we certainly didn't feel like what was beginning to be said or written about us. We always felt really good about what we were doing when we recorded and when we performed, and to a large extent, we didn't understand the kind of criticism we were getting." Lamm adds, "After *Critics' Choice*, I think everybody in the band got to the point where we felt like if we just try to do great work all the time, that will take care of itself. I'm not sure it ever did."

Lamm's complaint received a positive response in the *Billboard* review for the week ending June 6, 1973, which celebrated the growth of the band. "This band continues to progress in terms of musical expansion. Once it was the first band in the shadow of Blood, Sweat &Tears, combining rock tempos with jazz solos. Now it has become more vocally oriented, offering a pastoral sound which leads into temporal solos. It's nice to hear the sound of the horns, of course, but they aren't overpowering. All instruments play with a controlled exuberance, but it is the strength of the ensemble singing which shines through. 'In Terms of Two' almost sounds like a Gilbert O'Sullivan inspirational effort, with a harmonica adding a new trill to the band's blowing abilities. Best cuts:

FEELIN' STRONGER EVERY DAY

'Feelin' Stronger Every Day,' 'Hollywood,' 'Just You 'N Me.' Dealers: the band is riding on a new hot single, 'Feelin' Stronger Every Day,' so there is an awareness of Chicago." CHICAGO VI, recorded and released in the short month of February, debuted at Number 49 in *Billboard*. It would grab the Number 1 spot in July, eventually becoming the second most successful album of 1973, staying at Number 1 for three weeks before yielding to Jethro Tull's PASSION PLAY. Elton John took top honors with GOODBYE YELLOW BRICK ROAD.

Many things about CHICAGO VI are memorable. Most obvious, the album cover was printed using paper from the U.S. treasury — very appropriate, as this new incarnation of Chicago was definitely money in the bank . . . lots of money and lots of banks. A picture of the band, albeit a small one, was used above the logo, like a President's portrait would be on a bank note. Like CHICAGO V, this was also a single album, but the jacket swung open to reveal a large picture of the band members and their names. Someone may have realized that more people, especially young people, would buy the records if they knew who they were listening to and what they looked like. It worked. Chicago was gaining superstar status.

To help extend the visibility of the group, Dick Clark produced a television special for ABC called *Chicago in the Rockies*. Shot at Caribou Ranch, the program showed Chicago working in the recording studio, performing live for a crowd of friends and family at a cookout, and backing up singer Al Green. The performance with Green was certainly one of the show's high points. If nothing else, the telecast helped put names and faces to the boys in the band.

While CHICAGO VI may have left fans of the first five albums scratching their heads, a vast, new audience was coming on board. This new sound, look, and direction was easily embraced by a much larger demographic group. *Critics' Choice* was no *Introduction* or *Free*, but it was contemporary. Artists like Cat Stevens, Seals and Crofts, and Elton John were selling records and topping the charts, so to hear Robert Lamm sing an introspective, heart-felt piano ballad was in keeping with the times, though it may have shocked many of the band's fans who were probably expecting another *Hit by Varese*. Nonetheless, the album did show Chicago doing what they did best — blending myriad grooves, tempos, and idioms, though not in the abundance that was present in earlier recordings.

Perhaps the only tune to still convey that style was Lamm's *Hollywood*,

CHICAGO VI

a masterpiece. This is Chicago at its best. The band never sounded more unified. The song has all the raw power of *Free*, but is much more sophisticated and broader in scope. An interesting note about this album is the addition of Lee Loughnane as a vocalist singing the singular vocal part on Lamm's *Something In This City Changes People*. The song, which features three-part harmony throughout, works in conjunction with Lamm's *Hollywood* in showing obvious disdain for the whole L.A. scene at the time.

> People running everywhere
> Not one place to go
> Got no time to look around
> And find out where they are
> Where they are . . .
> Not getting anywhere
> Anywhere
> Hollywood crazy neighborhood
> Never understood why I stayed . . .
> — Robert Lamm, *Hollywood* (ASCAP)

Sophistication was certainly what the second single was all about. James Pankow's future classic, *Just You 'N Me*, became the most memorable tune of the album — became the quintessential Chicago song.

> You are my love of my life
> And you are my inspiration
> Just you 'n me, simple and free
> Baby, you're everything I've ever dreamed of . . .
> — James Pankow, *Just You 'N Me* (ASCAP)

Like *Saturday in the Park*, the tune can be enjoyed on many levels. On the surface, it is a beautiful ballad song that couples can dance to as they speak of their love for one another. With this song, Peter Cetera emerged as the ultimate lead singer for the band. But the song is also appealing to songwriters and musicians — lovers of jazz, pop, R&B, and what have you. The track featured some of Cetera's most memorable 'signature' bass work, as well as an instrumental section that gave way to Walter Parazaider's sinewy soprano sax solo, reminiscent of Traffic's *Low Spark of High Heeled Boys*. *Just You 'N Me* was

FEELIN' STRONGER EVERY DAY

a Number 4 hit in *Billboard* and Number 1 in *Cashbox*. And in response to the success of this single, CHICAGO V jumped back up to Number 1 in August 1973.

The band that resulted from the success of CHICAGO VI was a super-group. People loved the music and young musicians idolized the members of the band. Jimmy Haslip of the Yellowjackets, studio legend Nathan East, Bob Birch of Elton John's band, and session player Joe Iaquinto, for instance, have all heralded Cetera as a major influence in their bass playing careers. "Peter Cetera really floored me," says Joe Iaquinto. "When I first started playing bass in 1971, I was totally immersed in jazz and R&B. I didn't care for rock music. I especially didn't care for the tone of a lot of the rock guys' basses. When I joined my first band in 1973, the guys wanted to play Allman Brothers and Cream and Alice Cooper, and I would just roll my eyes and ask them for the chord changes. Then I would proceed to play jazz and funk lines! Finally, the guitar player took pity on me and recommended that I listen to Chicago. He was surprised that I hadn't heard of them yet. We went to his house and he played me the CTA album. I couldn't believe what I was hearing. It was everything that I was into, all at once. It was jazz with the R&B grease... and power! I was starting to get a bit bored with the jazz stuff I was listening to because I was a 13-year old boy and it just didn't give me the adrenaline rush and the outlet I needed at that age. But Chicago's music certainly provided that. I instantly became a huge fan, and I went from wanting to be Ron Carter when I grew up to wanting to be Peter Cetera. I even started singing, which I probably wouldn't have tried. Even though I eventually turned my ears towards Stanley Clarke and Jaco, as did most bassists in that era, I always came back to Cetera. His playing never failed to move me. 'Til this day, when I am called upon to create a bass line on record or in a live situation, there's a big part of me that thinks, 'What would Peter have played here?'"

Danny Seraphine was one of Buddy Rich's favorite drummers, respected as one of the elite. Terry Kath's name was synonymous with great guitar. New York session guitarist and jazz great, Jack Leone, has stated that Kath was the only rock guitar player out there doing anything of note. His solos and his rhythm work were what set Chicago apart from many bands that couldn't rise to their level. James Pankow, Lee Loughnane, and Walt Parazaider, the Chicago horn section, legitimized the instruments and made it hip for young people to play trombone, trumpet, and sax.

Despite the emergence of Peter Cetera as the 'voice' of Chicago, the band remained democratic in songwriting contributions. While Lamm penned five

CHICAGO VI

and a half of the tunes, singing four of them, Cetera's *In Terms of Two* kept his country folk side alive, and Kath's ode to his dog, *Jenny*, was true to form for the man who wrote *An Hour in the Shower*. With the success of *Just You 'N Me* and *Feelin' Stronger Every Day*, James Pankow made his presence felt as a songwriter, as he would increasingly on future albums. But for now, CHICAGO VII was on the burner and would spark a return to the double album and one of the most successful tours in history.

CHICAGO VII

COLUMBIA C2 32810

Danny Seraphine (drums, percussion) ∾ Peter Cetera (bass, vocals, guitar) ∾ Terry Kath (guitar, bass, vocals, bells) ∾ James Pankow (trombone) ∾ Walter Parazaider (tenor sax, flute, soprano sax, alto sax) ∾ Lee Loghnane (trumpet, flugelhorn, vocals) ∾ Robert Lamm (melotron, keyboards, Fender Rhodes, ARP synthesizer, piano, vocals, clavinet, Steinway) ∾ Laudir de Oliveira (percussion) ∾ David J. Wolinski (ARP synthesizer) ∾ Guille Garcia (congas) ∾ James William Guercio (bass, guitar) ∾ Ross Salamone (drums) ∾ The Pointer Sisters (background vocals) ∾ Carl Wilson (background vocals) ∾ Dennis Wilson (background vocals) ∾ Al Jardine (background vocals)

Side 1
Prelude To Aire
Aire
Devil's Sweet
Italian From New York
Hanky Panky
Life Saver
Happy Man
I've Been Searchin' (So Long)

Side 2
Mongonucleosis
Song Of The Evergreens
Byblos
Wishing You Were Here
Call On Me
Women Don't Want To Love Me
Skinny Boy

Perhaps it was the band's attempt to fight off the pop/rock star machine that made Chicago consider recording a jazz album in Fall 1973. If CHICAGO VII was to become a jazz record, though, Peter Cetera would have had to be led to it under protest. "I had just about had it with any more writing because the group was content with having the three writers," Cetera explains, "when three or four of the guys in the group had said, 'We're doing a jazz album next time, nothing but jazz songs.' I went, 'Hoo, boy,' and I think we tried that for a couple of weeks. That was the first time I could really talk to Guercio, and he goes, 'I hate this, this is not working,' and I said, 'Well, so do I.' He says, 'Alright, this is not gonna work, let's come up with a compromise.'" That compromise became one of the band's most revered collections, a double album supported by one of the most successful tours in rock history.

CHICAGO VII

CHICAGO VII continued the tradition of displaying the logo prominently on the cover, this time without the band's picture, in the form of an elaborately crafted, simulated tooled-leather-rendering, complete with illustrations of the famed Chicago fire-cow and the Chicago Stock Yards. Though the band wasn't featured on the cover, the gate-fold showed the band members (the "Chicago Seven", if you will) hanging out at the ranch.

Side one featured three instrumental tracks. The first, *Prelude To One*, written by Danny Seraphine, featured drums, percussion, and flute, with Robert Lamm adding color on a Melotron, a keyboard instrument popular in the '70s that emulated orchestral sounds by using dozens of tape-loops of real instruments. The second tune, *Aire*, written by Seraphine, Walter Parazaider, and James Pankow, contained a memorable melody played by the horn section with some great guitar work by Terry Kath, which *Guitar Player* recognized as "among the best Terry Kath on record. Terry, always exciting and creative, stretches out even more ... and Peter Cetera's bass is perfect." Side One's closer, *Devil's Sweet*, written by Seraphine with Walter Parazaider, was the drummer's dedication to two jazz greats, Jo and Elvin Jones, for their inspiration. This track was especially interesting, bordering on some of the great fusion albums of the early '70s, and very reminiscent of the Mahavishnu Orchestra and Larry Coryell's Eleventh House. The song also featured an ARP synthesizer solo played by David "Hawk" Wolinski, of the band Rufus. Wolinski and Seraphine would team up to write several songs for future Chicago albums.

With these "ambitious jazz-type pieces," as Parazaider put it, out of their system, Chicago proceeded to write and record some of their best pop music on CHICAGO VII. It's safe to say that the 'rock 'n' roll band with horns' was now becoming the 'pop band with horns'. Those skeptical about the acceptance of a half jazz, half pop, need only to look at the facts: CHICAGO VII was a hit with both jazz and pop fans, well-received critically in *Down Beat* and *Seventeen Magazine*.

In December 1973, *Seventeen*, a publication purely aimed at teenagers, published an article entitled "The Sound of Chicago: Bobby Lamm and Jim Pankow reveal what it's like on and offstage with a rock band." "Some of the fellows sport dark glasses, an occasional beard," the author comments in true *Seventeen* style. "Wearing multicolored outfits of sky blue, dark rose, red and black and yellow, they charge the latticework melodies with cheerful vitality." Robert Lamm is described as a "shaggy-haired keyboard man, featured vocalist and writer, whom the other musicians call Bobby," and "trombone man James

FEELIN' STRONGER EVERY DAY

Pankow, whose affable smile is as characteristic as his handsome mustache," receives they same glamorous treatment. Around the same time, Chicago was interviewed in *Down Beat*, a highly respected jazz publication in a feature entitled "The Chicago Papers," with the band members using expletives like "bullshit," and "fag" in response to the treatment they had been receiving from the press. Same band, two completely different representations, both accurate. A seventeen-year-old kid in the Midwest and a thirty-something jazz pianist in New York city, both fans of the same band, both buying the same record. The *Billboard* review of CHICAGO VII also caught this double focus of the album, favoring the pop over the jazz: "A lavish two-disk set, their latest will doubtless delight most fans with some exciting changes of pace, despite the occasional gaps that seem unavoidable whenever this act decides on a multi-disk approach. Some earnest jazz instrumentals seem least effective, but more familiar pop anthems, like 'Life Saver' and the new single, 'Searchin' So Long,' will sustain interest. Best moments come with a stunning assist from The Beach Boys on 'Wishing You Were Here,' with a closer runner-up to 'Skinny Boy,' featuring the Pointer Sisters." Here was Chicago, bridging the generation gap with their music. Perhaps the band, and certainly the press, didn't see it that way back then. But there you have it. And that is why CHICAGO VII worked.

The first single from the album, James Pankow's *I've Been Searchin' (So Long)*, was released in February 1974, a month prior to the album's release, which debuted in *Billboard* at Number 46. The album streaked to Number 1 on April 27, 1974. Pankow's beautiful ballad was about soul searching, a popular them in the '70s, as he recalls. "It was a song about finding myself, I was starting to figure out what I was put on this earth for. I don't think anybody in the band had written a song about the quest to meet that person inside and find out what he was all about, what his ideals were. I just had to talk about who I was and what I was feeling at the time. I felt after it was recorded that maybe other people could relate to that, cause the '70s was a time for soul searching. It was a time for discovery, and I think that song was probably indicative of what a lot of young people were feeling at that time."

> As my life goes on I believe
> Somehow something's changed
> Something deep inside, a part of me
> There's a strange new light in my eyes

CHICAGO VII

> Things I've never known
> Changing my life
> Changing me
> I've been searchin' so long to find an answer
> Now I know my life has meaning . . .
> —James Pankow, *I've Been Searchin' (So Long)* (ASCAP)

The song boasted a lush orchestral support track and a gorgeous vocal by Peter Cetera. There was even room at the song's end for Terry Kath to cut loose. *I've Been Searchin' (So Long)* would become the band's eighth Top 10 hit. As he did on CHICAGO VI, Peter Cetera came to the forefront to sing all the hits off the new album. It was evident that the bassist was gaining recognition as having one of the most recognizable voices in pop music, and a voice that was becoming synonymous with hit radio and records.

The second single, *Call On Me*, was written by Lee Loughnane, but not without some help. As Peter Cetera explains, "I tried to help Lee Loughnane with a song, and that song turned out to be *Call On Me*. Lee had written a song. It wasn't called *Call On Me*, it was called something else, and, in fact, it was terrible. I talked to him at the ranch one day, and he was all bent out of shape. He said that he had played the song for the guys, and that they had told him in fact to get the heck out of there with that song. I said 'well come on, let's have a go.' So Lee and I went and re-wrote the lyrics and rewrote the melody and came up with the song called *Call On Me*, which was a big hit for him." Loughnane remembers it a little differently. "Peter changed a couple of the words and the way he sang the melody in order for him to be able to play the bass and sing the melody at the same time because that's the way he felt it." Loughnane added, "I appreciate his efforts, and we did make the song a hit."

Call On Me, Cetera's *Happy Man*, and the instrumental *Mongonucleosis*, written by James Pankow, all had a Latin influence. Chicago had been working with Brazilian percussionist Laudir de Oliveira since CHICAGO VI, and he returned as a session player for VII. He would become a permanent member of the band before the close of 1974. "I used percussion a lot in the records to compliment the drums," noted Guercio. "I think Danny brought Laudir in, and we ended up using him quite a bit. He was a nice guy." "I met Laudir on a plane at the end of a tour," Seraphine recalls. "He was playing with Sergio Mendes at the time, and we had a great party on the plane with Bill Cosby. Then we didn't see him again for two or three years. We had already talked about adding

FEELIN' STRONGER EVERY DAY

somebody but couldn't really find anybody good enough to cover all of our music. We had found some guys who could cover the Latin stuff, but as soon as we'd get into other things, they'd just get all screwed up. Laudir just sort of complemented us; whatever was going on he could do. He could play anything, any type of percussion."

CHICAGO VII gave everybody in the band a chance to share the wealth and the spotlight. All seven people wrote at least one song on the double-disc, though Robert Lamm was, once again, the dominant writer with five cuts. Not only was the songwriting spread around, the playing and singing were as well. *Song Of The Evergreens*, one of two songs turned in by Terry Kath, featured Lee Loughnane on vocals. To some fans, there wasn't a big difference in the two singer's voices, and it went somewhat unnoticed. *Wishing You Were Here* featured Terry Kath singing the verses, but this was due to Cetera's mistake, more than anything else. "We recorded the musical track for *Wishing You Were Here* in a wrong key for my voice," Cetera recalls. "It actually should have been up a step, step and a half. For some reason, I just didn't realize that until after we had recorded it. So, therefore, that put the verses in such a low key that I just couldn't sing it, and that's how Terry got involved singing that one."

> Sleepless hours and dreamless nights and far aways
> Ooh-oo-ooh wishing you were here
> Heaven knows and lord it shows when I'm away
> Ooh-oo-ooh, wishing you were here...
> — Peter Cetera, *Wishing You Were Here* (ASCAP)

Terry also got involved as the bass player on several tracks: *Happy Man*, *Wishing You Were Here*, Kath's *Byblos*, and Robert Lamm's *Skinny Boy* were all supported by Kath's impressive bass work. Another bass player plugged in for CHICAGO VII, James William Guercio. Guercio actually studied the instrument while attending De Paul University. Guercio could be heard on Terry Kath's *Song Of The Evergreens* and he also played guitar on *Wishing You Were Here* and *Happy Man*.

The liner notes for CHICAGO VII had some unfamiliar names credited as musicians on Robert Lamm's *Skinny Boy*. That's because that track, sans the horn parts, was lifted from Lamm's ill-fated solo album. Released in August 1974, the album never made it onto the charts. The string arrangements were well done throughout, especially on the song *Temporary Jones*, and Robert's keys

CHICAGO VII

and vocals were very good. Terry Kath shined as the album's only bassist. His playing was as forceful and inventive as his guitar work. The album showed an intimate side of Robert Lamm and it took his offbeat quirkiness to a new level. It was that quirkiness that gave many of the Chicago records the levity necessary to keep them from being too overblown. Chicago fans may have been disappointed by the lack of horns on the album, but Lamm has always maintained that he felt CBS didn't support the record for fear that he would leave the band if he achieved solo success.

A last-minute contribution to the record, *Wishing You Were Here*, provided the launching pad for Chicago and The Beach Boys to begin their enormously successful tour. "There's two people that I always wanted to be," Cetera confessed, "and that was a Beatle or Beach Boy. I got to meet The Beach Boys at various times and got to be good friends with Carl Wilson. I remember I was living on the ocean, messing with the guitar one night, and the waves were rolling in, and I started learning that little lick that opens the song, and my then-lady was lying on the couch sleeping. We were going on the road within the next day or so, and with the waves coming in and that little lick, I wrote about the road."

By 1974, Chicago was everywhere on the road and in the media. Dick Clark produced a second special for ABC television, *Chicago: Meanwhile Back At The Ranch*. This time, the band was handled as if Clark were trying to turn them into the new Monkees. The music was secondary to the painful silent movie-era storyline that had guest stars Charlie Rich and Anne Murray interacting with Chicago. "It was bad," admits Robert Lamm. "Jimmy Guercio must have spent hours splicing all the tapes," he continues. "I know they shot better footage then what wound up appearing. So we found out what it's like to deal with the Dr. Pepper/ABC TV/Dick Clark mentality, which is totally noncreative." Danny Seraphine adds, "Anne Murray and Charlie Rich should have never been on the show. We got forced into that." The live footage of the band playing out-of-doors at the ranch was quite good, though . . . even when Chicago was relegated to being Anne Murray's backup band for her rendition of The Beatles' *You Won't See Me*.

Although CHICAGO VII was a hit among both jazz and pop fans, some critics continued to argue that the band had lost its way, abandoning their 'rock 'n' roll band with horns' roots for the more refined realm of jazz or for the more lucrative pop terrain. But wasn't the band allowed to grow, allowed to change? The Beatles were always changing. *She Loves You, Eleanor Rigby*,

FEELIN' STRONGER EVERY DAY

Yellow Submarine, and *I Am The Walrus* were not exactly cut from the same cloth. So it was with Chicago. The seventh album was most definitely a far cry from the first, second, or third, but it was the same band, the same songwriters. Any one band that can write *Beginnings, 25 Or 6 To 4, A Hit By Varese,* and *Saturday In The Park* should be lauded for their diversity, not condemned. Chicago was a seven-piece band with every member having a turn at bat. It was remarkable, if not astounding, that seven albums into their career, four of those being double albums, Chicago was constantly heading into new territory and coming out on top.

CHICAGO VIII

COLUMBIA PC 33100

Peter Cetera ~ Terry Kath ~ Robert Lamm ~ Lee Loughnane ~ James Pankow ~ Walter Parazaider ~ Danny Seraphine ~ Laudir de Oliveira ~ *Old Days* and *Brand New Love Affair* strings orchestrated by Pat Williams, *Harry Truman* vocal chorus by the Caribou Kitchenettes

Side 1
Anyway You Want
Brand New Love Affair —
    Parts I & II
Never Been In Love Before
Hideaway

Side 2
'Till We Meet Again
Harry Truman
Oh, Thank You Great Spirit
Long Time No See
Ain't It Blue?
Old Days

On August 1, 1974, Chicago went into production on their eighth album, this time with percussionist Laudir de Oliveira as a full-fledged member of the band. CHICAGO VIII was a single disc; in fact, there would be no more double albums for Chicago. Released in April 1975, the album debuted in *Billboard* at Number 14, the highest placing of any previous album, landing at Number 1 on May 3rd, holding this spot for two weeks before being bumped by Earth, Wind, & Fire, another band with a horn section. Albums in the Top 10 then included offerings by Led Zeppelin, John Denver, Olivia Newton John, Bob Dylan, Robin Trower, and John Lennon.

In the April 5, 1975 issue of *Billboard* magazine, Chicago was at last recognized for the diversity of their music and their sense of musical adventure: "This album aptly proves that Chicago will be around for many more years. They have stayed current in their compositions and, unlike many, they haven't keyed on one sound and made a career of it. True, they do have a trademarked sound, but that's in their use of horns. This album has some very fine moments and the group ably covers a number of musical areas. As usual the composer chair is shared by several group members and each is outstanding in its own way. . . . This group is a monster and the packaging suits them fine. The cover art will

FEELIN' STRONGER EVERY DAY

draw in eyes. Also, there is a poster included. Already on many of the nation's major radio stations, the cut culled from the 'CHICAGO VIII' LP is a highly commercial mix of nostalgia, horns and Beach Boy type harmonies. Almost certain to be charted within a week, and probably the strongest item the band has come up with since 'Saturday In The Park.'"

The album's first single, released in February, was Robert Lamm's *Harry Truman*, a Beatle-ish tune about the former president, and one of America's most trusted leaders. Timely, indeed, as the country was still reeling from the recently concluded Watergate-Nixon scandal. This was also the first Chicago single written and sung by Lamm since 1972's *Saturday in the Park*. Although he wrote four of the eleven tunes on CHICAGO VIII, Lamm felt that he was slowing down. "I think I was getting a little stagnant," Lamm admits. "We were partying pretty hard, too; there was a lot of drug abuse, a lot of alcohol abuse. That slowed us down. I was writing a little bit less, but not much less, and I think I was stuck creatively, so that even the things I wrote were mediocre, or not fully thought out. The touring schedule and the recording schedule really began to catch up to me, because I also wanted to have a life, and so I was really trying to figure out that balance, and it was not easy. For myself, those were the factors, but I also think that Peter began to write more and other members of the band began to write more."

Danny Seraphine was quoted in *Billboard's Book of Number One Albums* as saying, "I could never figure out to this day why the record company released *Harry Truman* in Japan. I think it ruined our career for a long time there." How true! Truman did, after all, order the atomic bombing of Hiroshima during World War II.

The second single from CHICAGO VIII, *Old Days*, also raced up the charts to Number 5 on June 7, 1975. Written by James Pankow, the song was a sentimental journey that closed the album and was, perhaps, what was on everyone's mind at that time. In hindsight, it seems that perhaps each person in the band, along with many of their fans, longed for the old days for a variety of reasons. Perhaps things had gotten too crazy, too out of control. As Pankow reminisces, "*Old Days* — it's a memorabilia song, it's about my childhood.... It touches on key phrases that, although they date me, are pretty right-on in terms of images of my childhood. The *Howdy Doody Show* on television and collecting baseball cards and comic books. Peter absolutely hated singing that song. He said, 'I'm not going out there and singin' "Howdy Doody," man! And "baseball cards and bluejeans." I mean, this is corny man.

CHICAGO VIII

I'm not singin' this shit!' And then we stopped doing it live, ultimately, because Peter refused to sing those lyrics."

> Old days
> Good times I remember
> Fun days
> Filled with simple pleasure
>
> Drive-in movies
> Comic books and blue jeans
> Howdy Doody
> Baseball cards and birthdays
> Take me back to a world gone away
> Memories seem like yesterday
>
> — James Pankow, *Old Days* (Big Elk Music/ASCAP)

CHICAGO VIII was perhaps the heaviest guitar album since CHICAGO V. Peter Cetera's *Anyway You Want* and *Hideaway* were a far cry from the soft sounds of *Wishing You Were Here* and *Happy Man*. Terry Kath's tribute to Jimi Hendrix, *Oh, Thank You Great Spirit*, featured some outstanding multi-tracked guitar work, as did Robert Lamm's *Ain't It Blue?* In fact, Terry Kath was in fine form on CHICAGO VIII. Having been temporarily pushed aside on the previous two albums, it seemed that Terry was back in the front line. His lead vocals on James Pankow's lush, organ-driven ballad, *Brand New Love Affair — Part I*, which featured a beautiful string part orchestrated by Pat Williams, were soulful and heartfelt. *Brand New Love Affair — Part II*, also by Pankow, switched gears and handed the groove-heavy track over to Peter Cetera, who sang of the new love with a growl in his voice that may have raised eyebrows among fans who had dismissed him as a ballad singer. Lamm turned in a beautiful ballad with *Never Been In Love Before*, sung by Peter Cetera, who also turned in a brilliant performance on bass, displaying his McCartney influence proudly. Lamm was also at his quirky best on the tune *Long Time No See*, which epitomized the growing pop rock sound of the band. For a man who felt that he was pretty well spent, Lamm still managed to keep Chicago's sonic identity alive, especially on *Ain't It Blue?*, the first song to incorporate lead vocals by Terry Kath and Peter Cetera since CHICAGO V's *Dialogue*.

In September 1975, a third single was pulled from the album, Pankow's

FEELIN' STRONGER EVERY DAY

Brand New Love Affair. Edited down from 4:31 to 2:30 minutes, the song failed to rise above Number 61. Was the public getting tired of Chicago constantly changing gears? Could it have been that songs like *Feelin' Stronger Every Day, Just You 'N Me, Call On Me,* and *Old Days* were the new sounds of Chicago's success? Could it be that a jazzy ballad sung by Terry Kath, even with a funky out-tro by Peter Cetera was not going to make the grade? That would have to remain to be seen. The album was a bit dark, the production a bit stiff, made by a bunch of guys who sounded like they needed to shave and take showers. And that's not necessarily a bad thing. If CHICAGO VI and VII sounded like the Caribou Ranch was softening the band, CHICAGO VIII was proof to the contrary.

To further insure the success of the album in the United States, Chicago hit the road for a 12-city tour with their CHICAGO VII teammates, The Beach Boys. The tour would gross over $7.5 million and play to well over 700,000 people. According to James Guercio, who was managing both acts, he had deliberately set up the tour to give Chicago a "kick in the ass," feeling that their concert programs, given over to hit medleys, had become complacent and sloppy. The Beach Boys, on the other hand, had, under Guercio's tutelage, become a renewed success with their ENDLESS SUMMER compilation of early '60s hits topping the charts, and Guercio had turned them into a tight, impressive stage act as well. The producer also went along on the tour as The Beach Boys bassist.

In sum, 1975 was an astonishing year for Chicago. They were truly at their peak. As of May 13, the band had six of their eight albums still on the charts.

CHICAGO IX

GREATEST HITS

COLUMBIA PC 33900

Peter Cetera ∿ James Pankow ∿ Walter Parazaider ∿ Terry Kath ∿ Robert Lamm ∿ Lee Loughnane ∿ Danny Seraphine ∿ Laudir de Oliveira ∿

Side 1
25 Or 6 To 4 (CHICAGO II)
Does Anybody Really Know
  What Time It Is? (CHICAGO II)
Colour My World (CHICAGO II)
Just You 'N Me (CHICAGO VI)
Saturday In The Park
  (CHICAGO V)

Side 2
Feelin' Stronger Every Day
  (CHICAGO VI)
Make Me Smile (CHICAGO II)
Wishing You Were Here
  (CHICAGO VII)
Call On Me (CHICAGO VII)
(I've Been) Searchin' So Long
  (CHICAGO VII)

Chicago went right back up to Number 1 with the November 1975 release of their first greatest hits package, CHICAGO IX. With sales in the United States alone of $4 million, this album became the band's biggest selling record. Released just in time for Christmas, CHICAGO IX entered the charts at Number 14 and steam rolled to Number 1 by December 13th, holding on until January 17, 1976, when it was bumped by Earth, Wind and Fire, the same band that took the spot from CHICAGO VIII a year earlier. *Billboard* had these kinds word for the package: "First greatest hits package for this all star group, one of the first to mix the sounds of rock and horns. While often considered an album oriented band, the seven have had their share of hit singles over the years, as this set aptly demonstrates. Equally impressive, they have scored with several kinds of songs — from jazz flavored to wild big band material to fun rockers to simpler tunes. The material has also covered a wide variety of subject matter. With the various musical feels and the fine combinations of lead and harmony vocals the group stands heads above most other 'supergroups' musically speaking — and, in fact, rank as one of the few legitimate American super bands."

FEELIN' STRONGER EVERY DAY

Dick Clark once again linked up with Chicago, this time having them host his *Rockin' New Year's Eve*. The band, decked out in tuxedos to bring in 1976, introduced the performers, including The Beach Boys, The Doobie Brothers, Olivia Newton John, and Herbie Hancock. Chicago themselves performed *Old Days, Harry Truman, Wishing You Were Here*, singing with The Beach Boys to a pre-recorded track for some reason, and closed the program with *Dialogue*. Chicago was joined on stage by everybody on the show to do the countdown to 1976 and to sing *Auld Lang Syne*, and then proceeded to play *Mongonucleosis* with an extended Latin jam that gave everyone, including Olivia Newton John, a chance to stretch out on percussion. (After recently viewing a re-run of the *Rockin' New Year's Eve* special, it was apparent that Peter Cetera did not, in fact, enjoy singing Pankow's *Old Days*. The singer virtually scowled through the whole performance.)

CHICAGO X

COLUMBIA 200

Terry Kath (guitar and vocals ⋙) ⋙ Peter Cetera (bass and vocals) ⋙ Robert Lamm (keyboards and vocals) ⋙ Laudir de Oliveira (percussion and vocals) ⋙ Lee Loughnane (trumpet and vocals) ⋙ James Pankow (trombone and vocals) ⋙ Danny Seraphine (drums and vocals) ⋙ Walter Parazaider (woodwinds and vocals)

Side 1
Once Or Twice
You Are On My Mind
Skin Tight
If You Leave Me Now
Together Again

Side 2
Another Rainy Day In New York City
Mama Mama
Scrapbook
Gently I'll Wake You
You Get It Up
Hope For Love

In March 1976, Chicago was back at the ranch starting to record their tenth album. CHICAGO X would become the album that changed the band forever. Although Chicago had seen five of their albums go to Number 1; they never had a single reach the top. *Saturday in the Park* came closest at Number 3. With the release of Peter Cetera's *If You Leave Me Now*, CHICAGO X would produce the band's first Number 1 single.

Picking up where CHICAGO VIII left off, the tenth album, the band's next original studio recording, offered more R&B songs, like James Pankow's *Skin Tight* and Robert Lamm's *Scrapbook*, a 3:29 summation of Chicago's career sung by Lamm, featuring one of the tightest, funkiest horn arrangements since *What's This World Comin' To?* from CHICAGO VI.

> Six sets smoked on Saturdays
> At Barnaby's on State
> Countless California calls
> We could not stand the wait

FEELIN' STRONGER EVERY DAY

We played the pier on Venice Beach
The crowd called out for more
Zappa and the Mothers next
We finished with a roar

Jimi was so kind to us
Had us on the tour
We got some education
Like we never got before ...

Lowdown at the Caribou
All rumors aside
Was we could never get together
Not unless we tried

Summer with The Beach Boys
We got sand in our shoes
Made some special music
Everybody sang the blues ...
— Robert Lamm, *Scrapbook* (ASCAP)

Terry Kath, who had turned in a great performance on CHICAGO VIII with his song *Oh Thank You, Great Spirit*, returned with another rocker, the album's opener, *Once Or Twice*. The song, a sort of Johnny B. Goode on steroids, gives Walter Parazaider a chance to blow his saxophone in the true spirit of the 'rock 'n' roll band with horns' he envisioned almost ten years earlier. Two more memorable tunes were Pankow's *You Are On My Mind* and Lee Loughnane's *Together Again*. Both songs featured the horn players as lead vocalists. Pankow's vocal performance came about reluctantly, however, when he felt that none of the other vocalists could sing it the way he heard it. "The reason I wound up singing," he explains, "is that they didn't make sense in terms of inflection and attitude until I went in there and said, 'Hey, guys, this is what I hear,' and Guercio said, 'You sing it!' I went, 'Oh, man, you're kidding,' — I had never sung a lead vocal in front of a mic in a studio before." The song would become part of Chicago's live set, with Pankow singing in the spotlight, as did Lee Loughnane on his contribution. All of this solidified Chicago's staunch democratic policy.

CHICAGO X

The first single from CHICAGO X was Robert Lamm's *Another Rainy Day In New York City*. The song had a Latin vibe complete with steel drums played by Othello Molineaux and Leroy Williams (Molineaux would go on to work with bass legend Jaco Pastorious) and a lead vocal by Peter Cetera that sounded like he was trying to imitate Ricky Ricardo. The song barely cracked the Top 40.

In July 1976, Peter Cetera's *If You Leave Me Now* was released as the second single. It was one of two ballads he had written for the album, the other being *Mama Mama*, an almost danceable track with a beautiful string arrangement. *If You Leave Me Now* almost didn't make it to vinyl, Cetera recalls. "That was one of those magical, 'Jeez guys, we need one more song' situations. In order to get everybody involved in it, which was probably one of the first times we had done it this way, I suggested that perhaps since Jimmy Guercio had learned the song from me, while I showed him the guitar part that I'd played, and he was a better guitar player than I was, that he should play acoustic guitar, and then we would let Terry play bass, Bobby would play piano, and Danny would play drums, and I would sing, and we would do it all together. 'Come on guys like the old days.' 'You mean we're gonna record all at once again?' And I said, 'I'll tell you what, I'll even kind of do it like a lounge singer. I'll take a mike and kind of walk around and show you guys where we're going with the song.' So, we learned the song, and that song as you hear it, was actually recorded live, albeit the vocal track was done over, just because I was walking around so much. I counted the song off, and we went into that groove, and what you hear is the song that we did. The only over dubs were the electric guitar that Terry put on later." Cetera forgot to mention the beautiful Jimmie Haskell string arrangement added to the song later on in Los Angeles, an arrangement that garnered the song one of its two Grammy awards.

Walter Parazaider remembers things a little differently, and his account also points up the piecework nature of the group's recording techniques by this time. "The rhythm section was really struggling over some song," he says. "Lee, Jimmy Pankow, and myself were done with our part of the recording. The foreman was taking us down to Denver to get us out of town. I remember Guercio and Peter talking, 'cause it was Peter's song, saying, 'If this doesn't work within the next couple of takes, we're gonna shine this. We've got enough tunes for the album.' I'm sitting around my pool three months later, and the local station goes, 'We've got the debut single by Chicago coming up! A song comes on. I'm cleaning my pool and I'm going, 'That's a catchy tune. Sorta sounds like McCartney. Where have I heard this before?' The next thing, they go, 'That's

FEELIN' STRONGER EVERY DAY

Chicago's latest release, *If You Leave Me Now*.' The main point of the story, outside of me being a dummy, is that, usually, things that just made the album end up being some of the biggest hits."

> **If you leave me now you'll take away the biggest part of me**
> **Ohh-ohh-ohh, no, baby please don't go . . .**
>
> — Peter Cetera, *If You Leave Me Now* (Polish Prince Music/ASCAP)

That the group didn't recognize the song's likely popularity is indicated by its decision to release *Another Rainy Day in New York City* as the first single. *If You Leave Me Now* came out at Number 45 but quickly streaked to Number 1, Chicago's first *Billboard* singles chart topper. CHICAGO X, itself, failed to top the charts, peaking at Number 3, but won the band its first of the newly minted platinum record awards, selling a million copies in three months, and spawning a third Top 50 single in Pankow's vocal debut, *You Are On My Mind*. The success of *If You Leave Me Now* overshadowed the album from which it came and also consolidated what, by now, seemed a definite preference on the part of radio, if not Chicago's audience in general, for lush ballads sung by Peter Cetera over any other style the band might care to put forward. The audience that had tuned into Chicago with hits like *Just You 'N Me*, *Feelin' Stronger Every Day*, *I've Been Searchin' (So Long)*, *Call On Me*, *Old Days*, and *Wishing You Were Here* had spoken, and their preference for Chicago songs, especially ballads, sung by Peter Cetera, became clear.

"Since *If You Leave Me Now* became a single, we've become victims of our own success," says James Pankow, who sees the impact continuing to this day. "Radio thinks of us as power ballads, period. If we give them an up-tempo song or we give them another kind of a groove, they won't play it because it's not what they hear as being Chicago." "To be sure, the 'ballad-ness' that the band became identified with through the singles after *If You Leave Me Now* — that drove me crazy," Robert Lamm comments. "I know it drove Terry crazy, because that isn't what we set out to be and it isn't how we heard ourselves, and it's still not how we think of ourselves."

For a number of possible reasons, CHICAGO X did not reach Number 1. Perhaps radio was again becoming less album-oriented and more singles-oriented. Or maybe the audience that bought *If You Leave Me Now* was less tolerant of the band's eclectic mix. A first-time listener hearing Peter Cetera singing *If You Leave Me Now* might be a bit turned off by a song like Robert

CHICAGO X

Lamm's *You Get It Up*. Conversely, if you were a Terry Kath fan, or you bought Chicago records to hear the horn section, you might have furrowed your brow upon hearing *If You Leave Me Now*. Peter Cetera had always shown Chicago's softer side . . . just not to this extent. Whatever your feelings, *If You Leave Me Now* was a smash hit, worldwide. The song sent Chicago on a world tour at the beginning of 1977. CHICAGO X went on to win the Grammy Award for Album of the Year, and *If You Leave Me Now* won two Grammys, for Best Arrangement Accompanying Vocals and Best Vocal Performance by a Duo, Group or Chorus. CHICAGO X also earned John Berg a Grammy for Best Album Package Album Design. When both sides of the "chocolate bar album," as it has been called by fans, where unfolded, the result was a giant candy bar with the Chicago logo exposed through the torn wrapper — the epitome of '70s marketing.

Just as CHICAGO V marked the end of one phase in Chicago's career, so did CHICAGO X. Only this time, the band faced a bolder challenge, and one that they may have felt no control over. Chicago had turned into a money factory for Columbia Records and the name of the game was sales. For a group of young men who based their professional lives on musical integrity, some serious soul searching was in order.

CHICAGO XI

COLUMBIA JC34860

Robert Lamm (keyboards, vocals, and percussion) ∿ Terry Kath (guitars, vocals, and percussion) ∿ James Pankow (trombone, vocals, keyboards, and percussion) ∿ Peter Cetera (bass and vocals) ∿ Lee Loughnane (trumpet and vocals) ∿ Walter Parazaider (woodwinds) ∿ Danny Seraphine (drums and percussion) ∿ Laudir de Oliveira (percussion)

Side 1
Mississippi Delta City Blues
Baby, What A Big Surprise
'Till The End Of Time
Policeman
Take Me Back To Chicago

Side 2
Vote For Me
Takin' It On Uptown
This Time
The Inner Struggles Of A Man
Prelude (Little One)
Little One

In April 1977, with the CHICAGO X world tour behind them, the band was back at the ranch to record CHICAGO XI. When they had completed this project, they took off once again for a full European tour, followed by another American tour. As Walter Parazaider recalls, eight years of constant touring "was taking a bit of a toll. We were getting pretty tired. We'd cut down the touring from 350 dates to 250, to 200, which is still a hell of a lot of days on the road, and I think at the end of some of the tours we were getting a little tired. Some of the shows could have been better, but let's face it, we were booming."

CHICAGO XI was released in September 1977 and hit the *Billboard* charts at Number 36 on October 1st (Fleetwood Mac's monumental RUMOURS album held the Number 1 spot) and was received with a rave review: "Chicago's newest represents the veteran group's most lushly orchestrated work yet. From the initial cut, the funky, often riveting jazz flavored arrangements maintain a thumping pitch, enhanced by the strong horn section. The complex rhythms and melodies fused with the tight brass and string arrangements produces a sound reflective of Chicago's jazzy pop approach to rock. The powerful vocals and harmonies, characteristic of past releases, is at its fervent peak as the

CHICAGO XI

material is mostly upbeat with a minimum of ballads. The funkified sound often displays the group's appreciation for R&B rhythms with its kick-it-out boogie feel. James Guercio's impeccable production again manages to highlight the distinct sound that has made Chicago a consistent platinum seller. The lyrics also rank among the strongest and together with the fluid orchestral arrangements, this is Chicago's most devastating album yet. Best cuts: 'Take Me Back To Chicago,' 'Little One,' 'Till The End Of Time,' 'This Time,' 'Mississippi Delta City Blues.' Dealers: Every Chicago album has gone platinum. This will be no exception."

Musically, CHICAGO XI was filled with an energy and a diversity that was reminiscent of the earlier records. Perhaps in defiance to the huge success of *If You Leave Me Now*, Chicago decided to follow up the 'chocolate bar' album with this 'edgier' collection.

CHICAGO XI contained some of Terry Kath's best work in years. The song *Mississippi Delta City Blues*, written by Kath in 1972 and included on their LIVE IN JAPAN album, sets the tone for a good portion of the record.

> I've got a laugh that I put on
> When I'm not at home, when I'm not alone
>
> And it's hard to fake that laugh
> When my insides are cryin'
> And my heart's torn in half
> And all the music I hear
> And the things I valued so dear
> Make me feel so blue
> They all remind me of you
>
> — Terry Kath, *Mississippi Delta City Blues* (Cook County Music/Big Elk Music)

Kath, who had been relegated to a supporting role since Chicago's leap to pop stardom, takes a commanding lead here, singing four of the eleven songs. His guitar work on his composition *Uptown* is raw, unbridled, closer to his 'live' playing than ever. And the multi-textured guitar solo on Lee Loughnane's *This Time* is brilliant, both musically and as a production.

Danny Seraphine, who had not been heard from since his instrumental offerings on CHICAGO II and prior to that on CHICAGO III with Lowdown, stepped out from the 'backline' to contribute some very memorable material to

FEELIN' STRONGER EVERY DAY

CHICAGO XI. Seraphine and his songwriting partner, David "Hawk" Wolinski, keyboardist from the band Rufus, came up with the soulful *Take Me Back To Chicago*, sung by Robert Lamm. The song is 'signature' for the band, with its mix of tempos and time-changes. Lamm, Seraphine, and Wolinski speak of returning to their hometown and eschewing the trappings of success for a simpler, more peaceful existence. This song would have a chilling meaning for all concerned over the months ahead.

> Take me back to Chicago
> Lay my soul to rest
> Where my life was free and easy
> Remember me at my best
>
> Take me back to Chicago
> Where my music was all I had
> I tried to be as good as I could
> And sometimes that made me sad
>
> — Danny Seraphine/David 'Hawk' Wolinski, *Take Me Back To Chicago*
> (Balloon Head Music/Big Elk Music/ASCAP)

Take Me Back To Chicago also featured Wolinsky's Rufus band mate and future funk diva, Chaka Khan, on additional vocals, listed as the "incredible preach at end" in the album's liner notes. (Chaka Khan would record a hit song duet with Peter Cetera fifteen years later.)

On CHICAGO XI, Robert Lamm was also back to waxing political, this time with his tongue-in-cheek *Vote For Me*, which featured a gospel choir, The Voices of Inspiration of Compton, from California. The song is about Lamm's bid for the Presidency. If nothing else, it's interesting to hear how the self-described 'revolutionary', who wrote about "tearing the system down" in CHICAGO V's *State Of The Union*, had lightened up by deciding to change the world by promoting consumer alternatives such as "new cars that run on beer."

The fact that Peter Cetera was only heard singing on one song for CHICAGO XI seems very odd given the success of *If You Leave Me Now*. It seems logical that the man who wrote the band's first Number 1 song and whose voice had delivered most of their big hits, should be given the biggest share of the spotlight, especially on the follow-up record. But Chicago didn't see it that way.

CHICAGO XI

Perhaps it was an act of defiance, or maybe just Chicago's system of democracy, that led to CHICAGO XI's focus on the rest of the band. Still, Cetera's one song on the album, *Baby, What A Big Surprise*, turned out to be the album's highest charting single. Lush orchestration, a high, tight vocal by Cetera, harmonies by Beach Boy Carl Wilson and Peter's brother, Tim Cetera, and a very Beatle-esque guitar solo all combined to take the song to Number 4.

> Right before my very eyes
> I thought that you were only fakin' it
> And like before my heart was takin' it
> Baby, what a big surprise
> Right before my very eyes...
> — Peter Cetera, *Baby, What A Big Surprise* (ASCAP)

It had been ten years and seven months since the first meeting of the band at Walter Parazaider's house, and Chicago was now one of the biggest American bands of all time. CHICAGO XI was certified platinum, and the album was given a positive review by the band's long-time nemesis, *Rolling Stone*, disproving Danny Seraphine's theory, which he explained in the 1974 *Down Beat* interview, "Maybe if we got a good review (from *Rolling Stone*), the album wouldn't sell. Then I'd really be worried." In the November 3, 1977 issue of *Rolling Stone*, reviewer John Swenson wrote: "Take a band of ambitious musicians, led by an R&B lounge-crooner keyboardist, a guitarist thoroughly influenced by Jimi Hendrix and a trombonist/arranger schooled in big-band swing, put them in the studio with a producer who understands their aspirations but wants to make three-minute hit singles, and you have Chicago. You also have several forces working against each other. Credit producer Jim Guercio with holding it together while realizing his goal, for Chicago has had more hit singles than almost any American rock group in the Seventies. Credit Bobby Lamm, Terry Kath, Jim Pankow and the rest of the band for taking direction and yielding to each other for the sake of equilibrium. Credit them, and while you're at it, listen to them, because CHICAGO XI is a triumph. Chicago has finally overcome its musical schizophrenia and come up with an album that balances musical direction with commercial demand."

In citing Guercio's ability in "holding it all together," this article, ironically but unintentionally, touched a nerve. Relations with Guercio had become strained to the breaking point. After ten years and eleven albums, Chicago would fire the man who had been referred to as their 'Svengali'. The split between group and manager had been a long time coming, with antipathy on both sides. "It started happening with the tenth record," says Walter Parazaider. "Things started getting pretty strained. He didn't want us to learn any of the production techniques. He'd go to sleep at nine o'clock, and we'd start producing the records ourselves. Or trying to. I think if you're the producer of your album, you have a fool for a client. You can't be that objective about what you're doing on both sides of the glass."

"I think basically we felt at that point that we had been used," says Peter Cetera. "We had signed contracts that we were told to sign . . . that we believed to be fair that weren't, and I think it was just utter frustration of being let down, 'cause here we are, a bunch of guys from Chicago that were honest and believed in people, and we found out that everything wasn't as kosher as we thought it was. The second reason is that, musically I think he'd had enough, and we'd had enough. We felt that he wasn't around to produce us anymore. He wanted to do other things, obviously, and we wanted to do other things with other people."

If Cetera criticizes Guercio as a producer, Robert Lamm notes that the band was also dissatisfied with him as a manager. "He wasn't ever our really hands-on manager," Lamm says. "Larry Fitzgerald was our hands-on manager. He was the guy that ran the office and talked to the promoters. Guercio owned the management company. Howard Kaufman, who now manages the band, was the business manager. Guercio had some kind of disagreement with these guys and fired them. Then he took on the actual management, or he tried to, himself, and that lasted just a few months, and then we fired him."

Not surprisingly, Guercio disputes these accounts, though he does not absolve himself from blame for the split. "You can't have that much control and not have people resent it after a while," he says. "I only intended to do it for a few albums. I did not intend to have it go on for ten records. If you really study the records, and you study the transitions of the albums, I'm pretty proud of all the records I made, 'cause they were not easy to make. As I look back, I was much too hard on these guys. I felt 'a thoroughbred by committee is a goddamn mule'. I gotta take the rap. I think I totally manipulated them for my own ends as well as theirs, whether they understood them or not." Guercio made it clear that the ends toward which he manipulated Chicago were broadly ambitious, in ways that the band could never have been expected to understand. "The only reason I made a commitment to contemporary music was because it was important to me to put Stravinsky, and to put Thelonious Monk, and to put Glenn Miller on the radio every ten minutes across the world," he says. It was to this end, he indicates, that he became involved in management and production. "The only thing that ever could manipulate me was a song, or a voice, or talent," he says. "That's all that ever moved me. The only ability I have, by the way, is I can make people twenty feet tall, if I see something special in them."

But at the height of their success, when Guercio was ready to take Chicago to a higher artistic peak, they disappointed him, he says. He recalls protracted arguments in which he told them, "You're breaking down the doors for all these other jazz musicians, classical musicians, to enter into the pop mainstream, and that's a sacred responsibility. So you got ten number one records. Great! What are you gonna do about it? Why aren't we doing an opera? Why aren't we doing a symphony? . . . That band achieved about 20 percent of what I thought it was capable of doing, and 10 percent of what I wanted it to do. . . . The music was no longer the basis of the relationship. It wasn't a creative enough process for me. The success could have continued, but I really needed to change what I was doing with my life."

In retrospect, it's not hard to see why the partnership, no matter how successful (and, perhaps, in part, because of its success) had to end. Guercio had exerted a powerful control over the members of Chicago, especially in the early days. And as they became stars, it seems inevitable that they would begin to chafe under his admittedly harsh leadership, even as they were eager to dispel the impression, prevalent in the press, that they were no more than enthralled Trilbys in the hands of a sinister Svengali. Guercio's final comment on the subject seems undeniable: "I was difficult to work with, but I knew what I was doing."

The dismissal of James William Guercio would not be the only fallout from the rigors of stardom and a decade of relentless pressures. Chicago was about to suffer a tragic personal loss that would force the band to emerge from the shadow of the logo and reveal their humanity.

On January 23, 1978, Terry Kath shot himself in the head and died. Contrary to what's been rumored, he was not playing 'Russian Roulette' and he was not at a party with other member's of Chicago present. Kath was sitting at the kitchen table of Chicago's keyboard tech, Don Johnson, cleaning his guns, and while waving one too close to his head, it went off and took his life.

"He was at my place the night before he died," remembers James Pankow. "He had been having major hassles with his old lady, and had been doing substances." Pankow claims that Kath had been awake for a couple of days before the incident. "He wasn't incredibly depressed, but he was bumming, and he was tired," says Pankow. "I said, 'Terry, do yourself a favor and lie down and get some sleep, man.'" Kath was a gun collector, an aficionado, and was heading out for the shooting range. He told Pankow that he was going to stay with Johnson after he went to the range.

Don Johnson was the sole witness to the shooting, but was not available for comment. Pankow offers his account of what happened. "He (Terry) loved shining his guns, taking them apart, and putting them back together. Evidently, he had gone to the shooting range, and he came back to Donny's apartment in Woodland Hills, and he was sitting at the kitchen table cleaning his guns. Donny remarked, 'Hey, man, you're really tired. Why don't you just put the guns down and go to bed.' Terry said, 'Don't worry about it,' and he showed Donny the gun. He said, 'Look, the clip's not even in it,' and he had the clip in one hand and the gun in the other. But evidently there was a bullet still in the chamber. He had taken the clip out of the gun, and the clip was empty. He put the clip back in, and he was waving the gun around his head. He said, 'What do you think I'm gonna do? Blow my brains out?' And just the pressure when he was waving the gun around the side of his head, the pressure of his finger on the trigger, released that round in the chamber. It went into the side of his head. He died instantly. Only Terry knows what he was thinking at that moment." Pankow emphasizes, "I do not believe, nor will I ever believe, that Terry was suicidal. Terry was a very strong individual, and he had never alluded to any notion of suicide, and Terry and I were very close."

Bob Ludwig recounts a chilling tale involving Kath and his guns. "I was living with Hank Steiger," Ludwig recalls. "The year was 1974." (Steiger, who still works for the band, has been a part of Chicago's road crew for thirty years; Ludwig had already left the band but was still very close to them). "We were sitting in the bedroom, me, my wife that I have now, and her daughter from a previous engagement, who was four or five. Her daughter gets up from her chair and sits in the bed. As soon as she sits down a bullet comes through the door and goes into the arm of the chair that she was just sitting in. All of a sudden the door opens and there's Hank, with a white face, looking at me in shock. What happened was that Terry had loaned Hank some guns. It turns out that this was the same gun Terry ended up killing himself with. It had a hair trigger, it would just go off. Hank was just outside playing with it and it went off. He was so distraught by this, he put the guns in the car and drove over to

CHICAGO XI

Terry's and told him that he never wanted to see the guns again."

Ludwig remembers Kath as total thrill-seeker. "He would always come over to our house with a gun stuck in his belt," says Bob. "He was a thrill-seeker, riding around on his motorcycle like a madman. He liked fast cars and guns. If he would have been thinner, he would have been into fast women, but he always had a problem with women because he was the heavy guy in the band and could never break that barrier. I think it kinda bothered him on one hand, but on the other hand, he loved to eat! He loved to party and stay up for days on end. He was a great guy. He was the spirit of the band, you might say. His influence on the band pushed them along. When he died, the band lost that push. He was almost in front pulling them, not so much behind and pushing. But probably a year or so before he died, he became very depressed and didn't know where he was going."

On an eerie note, the gate-fold photo for CHICAGO XI, taken by Reid Miles, shows Terry Kath being shot in the head by a policeman's bullet. Miles had provided photos of Chicago in various comedic chases with the law on the last four albums. This was the only one to involve gunplay. (Chicago's 'rock and roll mobsters' image became the subject of some controversy in 1979 when the *Wall Street Journal* published an article alleging that certain members of the band and their management had ties to the underworld.)

Terry Kath's funeral was held January 26, 1978 at Forest Lawn's Church of the Recessional in Glendale, California. The Associated Press published his obituary across the nation: "Governor Brown and 400 other friends and fans of Terry Kath gathered yesterday to mourn the death of the rock group Chicago's guitarist as selections from the band's latest album filled the mortuary chapel. Kath, 31, songwriter and lead guitarist for Chicago, died Monday night after pointing a loaded pistol at his head and pulling the trigger. His death was termed an accident by police investigators. In a service that resembled the huge Hollywood funerals given for movie stars, scores of fans — some weeping hysterically, some searching for a glimpse of a rock star — lined up outside Forest Lawn's Church of the Recessional and heard the service through a speaker system.

"Brown said after the service that he had come because 'He (Kath) was a good friend. He was a very good performer, a very good artist.' Among the mourners were Doc Severinsen and the other members of Chicago. After Chicago member Robert Lamm read a selection from Kahlil Gibran's *The Prophet,* a recording of Kath's haunting voice filled the chapel."

FEELIN' STRONGER EVERY DAY

"The Rev. Joe Burke, a friend of Kath's, stood in front of the guitarist's rose-draped open coffin and said, 'Someone said Terry's probably jamming with the late rock guitarist Jimi Hendrix right now ... I sure hope so.'" Kath is survived by his wife, Camelia, and his daughter, Michelle. He was to be cremated."

Prior to his death, Terry Kath's life had not been going well, as Pankow acknowledges. "He was an unhappy individual. His relationship was not going well. He was also certainly more dependent on chemicals than he should have been. He wasn't addicted to anything, but he was abusing drugs." That Kath may have been losing control was evident in contemporary group photos where he appeared bloated and disheveled. Concert footage from 1977 showed the once energetic guitarist looking stoic and lethargic.

Along with his troubled personal relationship and disenchantment with Chicago's direction, Terry Kath, according to James Pankow, was also dissatisfied with his standing as a guitarist. "He was unhappy because Jimi Hendrix and Jimmy Page, all the other guitar players were getting all the credit, and Terry Kath was a monster. He was making his guitar talk and making animal noises before Jimi Hendrix knew what he was doing. We were working clubs in Chicago, and Terry was banging his guitar against amplifiers and making it talk, and then the Jimi Hendrix Experience comes out, and this guy gets all the credit, and needless to say, Terry Kath idolized Jimi Hendrix. When we went on the road with him as his opening act, they spent hours together talking shop. But Terry never got credit for being probably one of the most inventive rock 'n' roll guitar players in history. The press overlooked him."

One of the few publications to recognize his innovative talent was *Guitar Player Magazine*, in a feature published in 1973, which serves as a fitting tribute to this musician: "In the ninth grade Terry got hold of a Kay guitar and amp, and took up with a local kid band, copying every Venture's record they could get their hands on. No gigs, but a lot of fun and experience. Three years later the self-taught guitarist felt it was time for some lessons, so he spent a year with a jazz teacher trying to learn to read chord patterns. 'He just kept wanting me to play good lead stuff,' Terry recalls, 'but then all I wanted to do was play those rock and roll chords....'

"As Chicago's lead singer and only guitarist, Terry Kath is probably the performer most easily identified with the band. His guitar sound has been called 'slippery, but with clear definition and a churning propelling beat' by one critic, 'bluesy' by another, 'damn fine rock and roll' by a third. Chicago trombonist

James Pankow says simply, 'He's the best soloist we have.' Though he doesn't read music, Terry manages to 'write' most of the band's charts. 'Actually, I just tell the guys what I want, maybe play the different parts, and then they just pick it up from there.' When one of the other members writes a tune, Terry's part has to be hummed to him. 'I have a pretty good ear,' he says, 'but I think it's starting to go from playing in front of the amp all the time.' Because the band developed by playing in one tiny bar after another, they are used to setting up close together on stage, and the only way Terry can hear what he is doing is by standing directly in front of his gear.

"Allied Electronics of Chicago made his 60-watt Knight amp. It has two speakers to get the sound he wants without being too loud. In concert, the amp goes through their custom-built PA system, which was designed by the people at Columbia Records. Terry says that the Acoustic Control people heard his amp, dug it, and designed the 150 series after it. Today Terry shares amp duties between the Knight and the Acoustic, depending on the sound of the auditorium they are playing. (Kath helped develop the Pignose portable practice amplifier. In 1972, he and several of Chicago's business associates started Pignose Industries. Kath eventually sold the company, which is still making Pignose amps to this day.)

"After the Kay guitar, he bought a Fender Stratocaster, which he still uses on the job. Thirteen other guitars have been acquired over the past few years, but it is the Stratocaster and a Les Paul Professional Gibson that he regularly uses. On the band's first LP, Terry played a Gibson SG double cutaway. 'The Stratocaster has the best vibrato, but I have trouble bending the strings without slipping off,' he says. 'But my hands are pretty strong, I guess from playing bass all those years.' He uses each guitar for different songs. Both utilize standard tunings.

"His stringing is highly unique. For the first, Terry uses a tenor guitar A. The rest is a Fender 10 set, with the Fender 1st being Terry's 2nd string, the Fender 2nd being Terry's 3rd and so on. 'I just toss away their 6th string.' He has tried some of the various ultra light gauges, but breaks them too easily. With his strength, he finds he has little trouble bending the heavier strings.

"Kath uses low action on both guitars, particularly the Fender, but isn't really sure he likes it. 'I like more grip. Like the strings to work against me, so I can really feel them when I'm getting into something.' The pick he uses is a Herco light gauge nylon. 'They're really unbreakable,' he claims. 'The only thing that ever happens is they eventually wear out. Sometimes I'll be playing

FEELIN' STRONGER EVERY DAY

along and find I'm missing the strings. I'll worry about it for days until I notice that the pick has worn down to half its size.' At first, Terry utilized a Basstone pedal that plugged into the guitar and had its own distortion. But now he uses a Cry Baby Wah-wah, 'but it breaks up a lot. They are all too distorted. None of them seem to get a good natural sound.'

"Anyone who has seen Chicago, has to admire the speed with which Terry plays. It's all-natural. No special techniques, no exercises. 'I just get all jacked up when we start cooking,' he says, 'and don't think about how I'm doing anything.' Normally he anchors his little finger to the guitar just below the strings. But when he's building one of those incredible solos, or rocking the entire band with an intensely strong rhythmic pattern, he just hammers away with his entire forearm. 'I'm too busy playing to worry about the movement or the fingerboard,' he muses. 'I just listen to it as it's all happening. . . .' Because of time, and maybe because he's playing so much, Terry doesn't practice guitar. 'I wish I did practice more,' he says half-heartedly. 'But mostly I play the jobs or when I'm working on a tune, I sit around and play drums. Got myself a set not too long ago.'

"It is surprising that a guitarist of his reputation and popularity hasn't been approached with free amps or guitars from assorted companies, but it's true. No one has ever offered to supply him with anything. If the Gibson people were to design a guitar to Terry's specifications, what would it be like? 'Well, first I'd want a better vibrato,' he states. 'Even the Bigsby's I've used haven't been good. They may make some great ones, but I haven't found them. You know, I'd like to be able to keep a chord in tune while dropping it an octave. And I'd like a longer neck, so I can move around on it. A neck with a heel that doesn't start until the 14th fret. Most guitars have necks that get fatter as you go up the fingerboard. That means you have to change your hand position as you play, and sometimes I'm really getting off, you know, and the fingerboard starts dragging my hand as I'm going up. About the only other thing I'd want would be a wider neck. My fingers are so fat that sometimes I deaden the string next to the one I'm fretting. Otherwise, everything's fine. My Gibson has a good clean sound, and I like my low impedance pickups. I haven't modified either guitar at all.'

"While he's dreaming about what he'd like, he gets into a couple of ideas he's trying to develop now. 'On *Free Form Guitar* I plug my Knight into a Dual Showman for an unusual effect. The Knight distorts when I crank it up, but the Showman keeps it so I can control the sound. But on a job, I can't stop

CHICAGO XI

everything after the tune and change back to my regular set up. So I'm working on having a foot pedal that will be able to change from one set up to the other immediately.' Terry is more hesitant about speaking of his other project. 'All I can say is that it's a machine that will get me a bowing effect, like if I was using a bow on a guitar — sort of. I'm not going to explain anymore than that, though, until I've got it built.' Kath likes to play long flowing lines, but Chicago's fans would hardly know it. 'Usually I solo on these wild tunes where I have to play as fast as I can. I get all jacked up on a gig, man, and I just can't slow down.' Terry, always interested in new effects, and in new ways to 'cook', tried playing slide for a short while, but never on record or in concert. 'I just couldn't seem to get anything going. After I'd play a few hours at home, I'd done all I could do with it. It was just too limiting for me.'

"Chicago's first album was produced in a week, with Terry sometimes playing a Stratocaster whose neck was held together with a radiator hose clamp. 'We just didn't have time. It was the same way on the second album. Prelude, a nearly symphonic piece with strings, woodwinds and brass, was a line I had in my head. We needed another tune so I played it for Peter Matz and he arranged and orchestrated it for some other guys to play....'

"The future looks pretty good for Terry Kath, ex-Dick Clarker, ex-Missing Link, ex-Big Thing. Commercially, Chicago can do no wrong. They sell out Carnegie Hall for a week, play before 20,000 at a time, see their albums sell a million dollars worth, even before they are released. And artistically, even the critics who once mistakenly called Chicago 'Another Blood, Sweat & Tears,' are realizing just how wrong they were, and just how creative and adventuresome this young band really is."

Fellow Chicago members are quick to acknowledge Terry Kath's extraordinary contribution to their adventure. "Terry was really a passionate element in the chemistry of the band, passionate and energetic and imaginative," says Robert Lamm, who calls Kath his best friend. "He was an original thinker. He was an inventor in many ways. He invented the way he played his guitar. He was the kind of guy that could probably teach himself to play almost any instrument. He had that ability to really work hard. So, in a band with as many pieces as this band had, for there to be only one guitar player, that's a big job, because he was playing rhythm and lead. I don't think there's ever been a better rhythm player. And then, Terry's leads are, for that day especially, world class stuff."

"Terry Kath was a great talent," says Jim Guercio, who worked with him on a solo album that was never completed. "The most supportive guy was Terry.

Terry's the big tragedy of the whole thing for me. He was the best guitar player. Hendrix idolized him. He was just totally committed to this band, and he could have been a monster [as a solo]. He never could get it together. The guy was the leader of the band. He had an incredible amount of talent. He had a great vocal potential. I knew him the longest. We grew up together."

Kath's death devastated Chicago. The band considered breaking up. "Right about there was probably what I felt was the end of the group," says Peter Cetera. "It seemed to me like that was a good point to end it all right there and begin again. Doc Severinsen, bandleader of *The Tonight Show*, was one of those who said, 'There's just too many people out there that would miss the music.' I don't know, I think we were a bit scared about going our separate ways anyhow, and we decided to give it a go again. It wasn't the easiest thing I had ever done."

CHICAGO XII

HOT STREETS

CK 35512

Peter Cetera (bass, guitar, vocals) ᛫ Donnie Dacus (guitar, vocals) ᛫ Laudir de Oliveira (percussion) ᛫ Lee Loughnane (trumpet, vocals) ᛫ James Pankow (trombone) ᛫ Danny Seraphine (drums) ᛫ Robert Lamm (keyboards) ᛫ Walter Parazaider (woodwinds)

Side 1
Alive Again
The Greatest Love On Earth
Little Miss Lovin'
Hot Streets
Take A Chance

Side 2
Gone Long Gone
Ain't It Time
Love Was New
No Tell Lover
Show Me the Way

The October 16, 1978 edition of *People Magazine* (published in Chicago) included the headline, "In a Year of Grief, the Band that Made Chicago Famous Comes Alive Again." You could say whatever you want about Chicago, but they certainly don't let the grass grow under their feet. Four months after Terry Kath's death, the band had a new manager, a new producer, a new guitarist, a new image, and was in the recording studio working on their twelfth album. Their tribute to Terry Kath, *Alive Again*, would be the first single released from the album.

As the *People* article noted, for the closely-knit eight-member group, *Alive Again* is more than just a title. "Last January lead guitarist Terry Kath, at 31, accidentally killed himself while fooling with a 9-mm. automatic pistol he assumed was empty. Though Kath's tragic death was the result of recklessness, not any rock star death wish, 'it hit us all like a wall,' says vocalist/bassist Peter Cetera. 'The bottom really fell out. We thought, is this the end of the line?' Keyboardist Robert Lamm recalls: 'We were on the ropes emotionally and psychologically. We couldn't imagine standing onstage without him.'" The article goes on to discuss the break between the band and James Guercio, quoting Robert Lamm as saying, "We were naive and idealistic and stuck to the

FEELIN' STRONGER EVERY DAY

music. Jimmy produced some great albums and encouraged and supported us financially in the beginning. But then he got up on a mountain and gave directives. It didn't wear well." To compound these problems facing the band, they began to re-examine their image. "As a result of our marketing campaign," Lamm noted, "the band still had no image at all as we were getting into our 30s. We felt that maybe we should have some control. Terry's dying caused us to evaluate our lives." Lamm went on to explain the band's decision to carry on, a decision their friend Doc Severinson encouraged: "You have changed my life and others with your music, and you have a tremendous responsibility to continue," Lamm recalls Severinson urging. "It sounds banal and ridiculous, but we felt that everything that Terry worked for — whatever we had left of him — would be lost otherwise." Lee Loughnane felt an even deeper sense of obligation: "I feel he's watching us up there right now."

Peter Cetera talks about filling Kath's void. "We were looking for anything at that time. We thought what we needed was a young guitar player with long hair. One of the worst things you can do is interview new people, and that's what we had to do. We sat through I don't know how many guitar players; it seemed like a thousand, but I'm sure it was 30, 40, or 50 guitar players. Right toward the end of our tether, Donnie Dacus showed up, and we weren't really in any proper frame of mind; everybody was so fed up with interviewing people and listening to different guitar players try and play our stuff. Donnie Dacus actually had practiced a bit and came and played a couple of songs right and with fire, and we thought, 'Why, my God, he's got long hair, let's go,' and that's how he was in the group." As Robert Lamm told *People*, "he just burned on everything. He blew us away. The kid's an original." Cetera recognized that Dacus would bring to the band a new flair, a different feel. We were getting stale. He's a real rocker. It was like being born again." That Chicago would think they needed to replace Kath with a 'rock' personality seemed very odd. Perhaps they felt that James Guercio had kept their identities obscured behind the Chicago logo for so long that now was the time to be the rock stars they supposedly were.

"We weren't necessarily looking for someone to sing like Terry," Robert Lamm explains. "We were looking for someone to knock us out, and Donnie did." He was everything that Terry Kath wasn't. Skinny, blond, with a tenor voice and a playing style that puzzled many who were expecting a guitarist at least of the same caliber as Kath. While he tried to emulate Kath's rhythm patterns, he couldn't come close to Kath's soloing prowess. But that did not

CHICAGO XII

seem to be what Chicago was interested in. Live, Dacus was a showman. He moved all over the stage, wildly swinging his Peter Frampton-ish hair. He certainly added a visual dynamic that the band had never had before. Maybe Chicago was oblivious to the fact that their audience accepted them for who they were, and did not attend their concerts to see them leap about, but rather to enjoy the music and relate to their common-man demeanor.

Donnie Dacus was a young Texan with puppy-dog eagerness and fashionably long, shaggy blond hair. His laudable rock credentials included tenures with Stephen Stills, Boz Scaggs, and Kiki Dee. The cornerstone of his reputation is the three and a half years he spent working with Stills, a period that ended bitterly, however. "Some horrible things happened between Stills and me," Dacus recalled. "I didn't think I was getting what I deserved in terms of credit for my songwriting and advancement in the band. And I didn't have much freedom. It was a drag, man. Chicago plays a whole spectrum of sound but Stills plays only one thing." After splitting with Stills in 1975, Dacus worked in several bands and then drifted into a role in Milos Foreman's film version of *Hair*, scheduled for February release. Though he had no acting aspirations, Dacus accompanied a friend to an audition for the movie. "I went as a joke," Dacus recalls. "I never thought I'd wind up with a part. It was a fluke." Dacus was performing with *Hair* when another friend told him about the Chicago auditions. Though it angered the filmmakers, Dacus left the movie location to go to the tryouts. He finished the 23-week shooting schedule in May, just in time to begin recording the Chicago album.

With Dacus in place, Chicago recruited Phil Ramon to co-produce the album with the band members. Ramon had worked with the band for many years, mixing CHICAGO VI, VII, and VIII. He is best known for his work with Billy Joel. As the credits for the album show, the album was recorded, engineered, and produced by many hands in many studios in many cities. Gone was the unity and simplicity offered by Caribou Ranch. With the change in producers and image came a new band manager, Jeff Wald, whose clients included his wife, Helen Reddy, Flip Wilson, and Sylvester Stallone.

Perhaps the most notable thing about the album was its title — it actually had one! HOT STREETS became the first Chicago record to have a name and not a numeral. Surely this was the band's way of showing their independence from Guercio and his numbering system. Another first was the appearance of the band members on the cover. With the exception of the tiny head shots on CHICAGO VI, the logo was always the star. The logo was still on the cover, but it

FEELIN' STRONGER EVERY DAY

was reduced to a supporting role. "We wound up doing a survey," says James Pankow, "and 90% of the people surveyed [didn't give] a shit about what we looked like, much to our chagrin. They wanted to see the logo. The music has always spoken for itself, and the logo has as well. It's like Coca-Cola; when you see it, you know what it is. So we had to put our ego in a bag and bury it in the front lawn."

This new look immediately prompted a response from the music media. Freelance reviewer Henry Kujawa had this to say about the 'new band'. "I remember walking by this in the record store when it first came out, and suddenly realizing it was a new Chicago album! The shrunken logo and the members cavorting on a white background (perhaps 'inspired' by the similar cover to Earth, Wind & Fire's THAT'S THE WAY OF THE WORLD?) seemed a drastic way of saying, 'This is a new Chicago.' But even on first listen, any fears were put aside. Despite the loss of Terry Kath, this album maintained the sound and style of many of its predecessors (especially CHICAGO VI, VIII, and IX). While nowhere near my favorite, I've always enjoyed it. Highlights for me have long been *Alive Again*, *Gone Long Gone* (somehow the intro riff on this always reminded me of George Harrison's playing), and *Little Miss Lovin'* (their duet with The Bee Gees!). Listening to it now, it strikes me that a few songs on this sound like they came off a Billy Joel album — I guess his *The Stranger* had a big effect on his contemporaries." The new Chicago even looked different. Gone were the gold lame outfits, space suits and capes, and rhinestone jackets. Now, the band was wearing designer suits and looking very GQ (*Gentlemen's Quarterly*). Where the Chicago of yesterday was bigger than life, a troop of mystery men beneath the glowing logo, this new band was human, accessible, and scaled down to less mythical proportions.

The band also began opening up to the media, exposing their private personal lives. As *People* reported in characteristic style, "all eight musicians live in relative tranquility between the suburban plushness of Bel Air and the wilder contours of Zuma Beach. Rather than cruise with the Hollywood & Vinyl crowd, they visit among themselves. Rehearsals are in a small studio at Seraphine's house, where the driveway fills up with Lamm's VW, Loughnane's Aston Martin, assorted Mercedes and Porsches and the matching Rolls-Royces of Pankow and Parazaider. 'We once thought making it was affording cashmere suits,' muses Pankow. 'If you had told me back then that we'd someday own matching Rolls, I'd have laughed — or puked.' With five wives, two live-in 'old ladies' and nine kids among them, Chicago is more a family than anything else.

CHICAGO XII

Lamm's second wife, Julie Nini, is the younger sister of Cetera's girlfriend of six years, Diane. Terry Kath's lady, Camilla, is still a 'sister' to the group, and recently she joined them during an image-polishing stand in New York's Central Park. And when the wife of a road manager died last month in a car crash, band members rendezvoused from distant vacation spots to be with him at the funeral. 'We honestly love each other as brothers,' says Pankow of the egalitarian group. 'We don't let anybody get out of hand. If someone feels insecure — that he isn't needed in this band, and we have all felt that way — the others are there to give him strength.'" Band members even went so far as to discuss their financial affairs, how they created a group pension fund to invest one-quarter of their revenues. "That eliminated money as a reason to break up," Robert Lamm noted. "We'd all have hundreds of thousands of dollars left, even if everything were to dry up tomorrow." As Walter Parazaider summed up their lives for *People*, "here there's no backbiting or jealousies... This is utopia, the best of everything. If you can't keep your sanity, then all those gold and platinum records don't mean anything."

As Chicago records go, HOT STREETS sounded right. You might think that with Guercio gone, the band would have gone completely left of center, but that wasn't the case. Instead, they proceeded in kind, but with a remarkable sense of freedom and energy that came shining through on every song. Peter Cetera's voice was up front in the mix, all his emotions going to tape like never before. His bass playing sounded inspired once again, as if he had rediscovered the instrument. And it wasn't just Cetera. The whole band played and sang like a great weight had been lifted from them. After one listen to HOT STREETS, it was apparent that Guercio had definitely turned certain knobs the other way from where the band would have had them.

James Pankow introduced the new Chicago to the world on side one of the record with his song *Alive Again*. The title obviously alludes to the band's resurrection from the devastating loss of Terry Kath, but with so many beginnings and endings for the band, all happening at once, it could be taken a number of ways. Pankow makes it simple. "Lyrically, on the surface, it's a relationship. I used a relationship as a vehicle. If you read between the lines, it's a tribute to Terry Kath's passing, and the fact that we've got the ball. That's the first song we recorded subsequent to Terry's death. It's the band saying that we're alive again and we have a new lease on life, and Terry's looking down on us with a big smile."

FEELIN' STRONGER EVERY DAY

> Yesterday I would not have believed
> That tomorrow the sun would shine
> Then one day you came into my life
> I am alive again
>
> — James Pankow, *Alive Again* (Make Me Smile Music/ASCAP)

There is a guitar solo at the end of *Alive Again* that has Donnie Dacus trying his best to sound like Kath, wah-wah pedal and all. Since the song was meant as a tribute, it must have seemed like the right thing to do. But overall, for those of us who were big fans, Terry Kath's presence was sorely missed on HOT STREETS.

The rest of the album was split up among the remaining writers. Danny Seraphine and David 'Hawk' Wolinski continued their CHICAGO XI partnership and contributed two songs, *The Greatest Love On Earth* and *Show Me The Way*. The former is an almost R&B ballad that gives Peter Cetera the perfect opportunity to use his emancipated vocal talents to their fullest extent. Cetera's performance made it clear that he was truly one of the greatest singers in pop music, not just the bass player who sang the tenor parts. *Show Me The Way* is a quirky tune with the requisite tempo changes and genre-hopping that Chicago is famous for. Robert Lamm is the lead vocalist here, showing a lot more range than usual. With Terry Kath gone, Lamm was now the band's only baritone voice. His harmonic interplay with Cetera, which had always been enjoyable, was crucial now.

Lamm, himself, penned only two songs for HOT STREETS: the title track, which sounded like a companion piece to CHICAGO X's *Another Rainy Day In New York City*, and *Love Was New*, which showed him at his romantic best. In fact, with the exception of Robert Lamm's *Love Song* on his solo album, *Love Was New* could very well have been Lamm's best love song to date. The song should have been released as a single.

The new-kid-in-town, Donnie Dacus, took his shot with *Ain't It Time*, co-written with Danny Seraphine and W. Shebke, and driven by a unison guitar and bass riff. The song lets Dacus sing the story of how he got his big break. The bridge is classic rock with the horns coming in on the action, and Peter Cetera growling like the rock singer we always knew he was. Dacus manages some interesting multi-layered, effects-laden guitar work. Dacus gets another turn at lead vocals on Lee Loughnane's *Take A Chance*. After eleven albums with Kath, Lamm, and Cetera, it is difficult to accept a strange voice,

CHICAGO XII

but Dacus steps up to the plate and delivers respectably. Unfortunately, the song ends with an extended guitar solo over a high-octane tempo change that serves as a stark reminder of the void left by Kath.

Peter Cetera's contributions came in the form of his own riff-heavy rocker, *Little Miss Lovin'*, and the country-meets-McCartney song, *Gone Long Gone*. In a review of HOT STREETS, *Circus* magazine slammed *Little Miss Lovin'*, arguing that "an aging Peter Cetera lusting after a sixteen-year-old in tight blue jeans" was hard to take. (Mick Jagger and Steven Tyler could still be accused of the same sin.) The magazine also bashed *Little Miss Lovin'* for the presence of the Bee Gees, saying that their backing vocals added "unintelligible funkisms" to the song.

Cetera, Loughnane, and Seraphine created the album's most memorable and frequently played hit, *No Tell Lover*. With its tight, lush harmonies, R&B flavored rhythm track, and optimum use of the horn section, *No Tell Lover* became an instant Chicago classic.

> Pretty smile, lovely face and a warm breeze
> Now I need you lady
> You're my no tell lover
>
> Every night in a different place
> I'll meet you tender lady
> You're my no tell lover
> — Lee Loughnane/Danny Seraphine/Peter Cetera, *No Tell Lover* (ASCAP)

HOT STREETS was a respectable comeback album for a band that had a lot to come back from. While the production and the material may not have had the depth and mass of the Guercio/Kath era, this new formula was truer to Chicago's live sound, which had always been more unbridled than their recordings. The band had high expectations for the album as Peter Cetera told *People*. "We're still waiting for the Big One — five million. If this one doesn't do it, nothing will." But the album was less successful on the charts than previous efforts: the only song to hit the charts was *Alive Again* which entered *Billboard*'s Top 100 on the week ending October 21, 1978 at Number 63 and peaked on December 9th at Number 14, the same rank achieved by *No Tell Lover*. The album failed to make the Top 10, peaking at Number 12. Nevertheless, the

FEELIN' STRONGER EVERY DAY

critics at *Billboard* stated that "Chicago's 12th album should continue the broad commercial acceptance it achieved with its first 11 LPs, and also restore the group's critical acceptance, which has been sagging in recent years."

CHICAGO XII

"What PIGNOSE® offers, you can't refuse."

That's Terry Kath, the lead guitarist with Chicago.

He may not be a "Godfather" but he's a *gangster* on guitar. As a talented member of a great band, Terry's sphere of influence is very large—it reaches around the world.

At Pignose Industries we can appreciate that kind of influence. So we offer Pignose, the amp that offers freedom at last for the electric guitar.

Pignose is an *extremely* portable guitar amplifier. It runs on six penlight batteries or regular AC house current.

But the most important feature of any amplifier is the way it sounds. Pignose *really* puts out. The sound is tough, mellow and very legendary among the pros.

To the student musician, Pignose is a sensible, economical alternative to those big, fat, clumsy amps that always seem to end up in a corner looking old and tired. Instead, Pignose is a ready companion for you and your guitar. It *never* outlives its usefulness.

The sturdy construction, incredible sound, and tasty styling all add up to make Pignose the ideal amplifier for traveling, recording or just plain jamming-with-friends.

And for only $89.50 (suggested retail price) you can't refuse.

International Distribution by the CF Martin Organisation, Nazareth, Pa.

FEELIN' STRONGER EVERY DAY

CHICAGO 13 Tour: Peter Cetera and Laudir de Oliveira (top), Robert Lamm and Donnie Dacus (bottom).

CHICAGO XII

Danny Seraphine (top) and the Chicago horns with Chris Pinnick on guitar (bottom).

FEELIN' STRONGER EVERY DAY

CHICAGO 16 Tour: Peter Cetera and Danny Seraphine (top), Peter Cetera, Robert Lamm, and Bill Champlin (bottom).

CHICAGO XII

Bill Champlin (top),
James Pankow (left),
Robert Lamm (right).

FEELIN' STRONGER EVERY DAY

Robert Lamm with Bob Ludwig's custom microphone stand (top) and Peter Cetera (bottom), 1985.

CHICAGO XII

FEELIN' STRONGER EVERY DAY

Peter Cetera, CHICAGO 17 Tour.

CHICAGO XIII

COLUMBIA FC36105

Robert Lamm ∾ Peter Cetera ∾ Donnie Dacus ∾ Danny Seraphine ∾
Walter Parazaider ∾ James Pankow ∾ Lee Loughnane ∾ Laudir de Oliveira

∾

Guest Appearances by: Maynard Ferguson, Airto Moreira,
David "Hawk" Wolinski.

Side 1
Street Player
Mama Take
Must Have Been Crazy
Window Dreamin'
Paradise Alley

Side 2
Aloha Mama
Reruns
Loser With A Broken Heart
Life Is What It Is
Run Away

While *Billboard* saw a return to critical acceptance for Chicago with the release of HOT STREETS, *Rolling Stone*'s Jon Young held a different opinion of their next album, CHICAGO 13. "After one album without a number for a title, Chicago reverted to its practice of tagging releases like so many pieces off the assembly line," Young wrote. "This gauche move isn't the only aspect of 13 that invites derision: the band consistently displays such an un-ironic 'have a nice day' attitude that you begin to entertain suspicions it's gone prematurely senile.

"But Chicago hasn't degenerated. These musicians are simply employing the same hokey tricks they always did. 'Street Player,' the endless ramble that opens side one, uses an extended rhythm passage and bellowing horns for no discernable purpose besides padding. 'Aloha Mama' and 'Mama Take are the sort of glib jive that's ultimately patronizing. 'Run Away,' an ode to escapism, serves as an unpleasant reminder of what happened to all of the free-spirit tenets Chicago had once parroted so proudly. Robert Lamm's 'Reruns' is a rare example of the group severely restricting its scope and coming up with a passable romantic bonbon. Otherwise, Chicago's art is the usual cosmetic affair:

FEELIN' STRONGER EVERY DAY

A Stevie Wonder inflection in the profoundly titled 'Life Is What It Is' means class. Donnie Dacus playing guitar with surly lethargy in 'Must Have Been Crazy' equals rock & roll. Guest shots from Maynard Ferguson and Airto Moreira result in jazz. Yet, for all the bland (and ineffective) calculation, it's hard to find this band offensive; it doesn't exhibit enough smarts for that. Because they're too stupefying to be taken seriously — the only people these guys are likely to fool are themselves."

Billboard was somewhat more benevolent, but uncharacteristically reserved in an August 18, 1979 review. "Obviously disheartened by criticism in recent years that the band has gone soft, there is more of a rock, blues and soul feel to this new Chicago effort. There is only one ballad ('Loser With A Broken Heart') but even this is delivered with punch. Fans of the straightforward Chicago will find 'Street Player' and 'Mama Take' more in keeping with the standard Chicago sound. The other eight cuts, however, show a distinct return to rock basics. Those who were hoping the group would go in a jazz direction will be disappointed, as jazz is not emphasized. Instrumentation, vocals and production are as seamless as ever."

Business as usual for Chicago! The critics divided, like the music, among rock, pop, and jazz.

Recorded in Montreal, Canada, and Los Angeles, California, in May 1979, CHICAGO 13 (gone were the roman numerals) once again teamed the band with producer Phil Ramon. The album features songs by everyone in the band. Even Walter Parazaider, who had only once before been given a writing credit for the instrumentals *Aire* and *Devils' Sweet* from CHICAGO VII. "When we hit the thirteenth album, everybody was writing, and I think everybody got a song on that album," Parazaider states. "I'd have to say that album could have been conceptually a little disjointed, although I think the material was good." Parazaider's contribution was the bluesy *Window Dreaming*. The song, co-written by Lee Loughnane, featured Peter Cetera singing as "P.C. Moblee, courtesy of the Peter Cetera Vocal Company." That song, along with Danny Seraphine and 'Hawk' Wolinski's *Aloha Mama*, had Cetera/Moblee using a gutsy, beefier set of vocal pipes that seemed to be trying to make up for the part of the spectrum left vacant since Terry Kath's demise. It was an interesting and ambitious effort by Cetera to give the record a unique sound, which also gave Cetera a chance to stretch out vocally. Cetera wound up singing seven of the album's ten songs. He also wrote two songs: *Mama Take*, an acoustic guitar-driven tune that sounded like Cat Stevens at his best, and the very

CHICAGO XIII

McCartney-inspired *Loser With A Broken Heart*.

Robert Lamm's voice was heard only once in lead vocal capacity, fronting one of his two offerings, *Reruns*. The song had a Fleetwood Mac quality with an extremely infectious chorus, and should have been released and pushed as a single. Donnie Dacus' entry, *Must Have Been Crazy*, was released as the single but barely made the charts, peaking at Number 83. The decision to release *Must Have Been Crazy* may have been prompted by Chicago trying to make the new member of the band feel like an equal partner. Another song which seems like an obvious choice for a single, in hindsight, was percussionist Laudir de Oliveira and Marcus Valle's *Life Is What It Is*. The song had all the components for a successful Chicago tune: a beautiful melody sung by Cetera, plenty of harmonies, and a strong support track by the horn section.

For the first time in their long career, Chicago seemed to be foundering on the high charts. The band that once stood head and shoulders above the one-hit-wonders and flavor-of-the-month fads so prevalent in the music industry was becoming a victim of it's own autonomy. As the 1970s came to a close, disco music had pushed a lot of rock and pop bands off the charts and out of the limelight, sophisticated bands like Chicago and Yes. Rock bands like Grand Funk Railroad were feeling the bite, too. "Grand Funk did not disco," said Mark Farner in a VH1 interview. "We would not bow our knee to the God of disco," he said, offering the explanation for why Grand Funk Railroad packed it in. But Chicago was not about to give up. Instead of fighting or surrendering to the genre, the band decided to join in. Chicago's entrance into disco music, *Street Player*, rose to Number 21 on the charts in August. "*Street Player* was our two cents' worth for disco," says James Pankow. "We wanted to get on the radio, but it really didn't do anything. But I thought it was a relatively intelligent approach to disco." *Street Player* was written by Danny Seraphine and 'Hawk' Wolinski, recorded by Wolinski's band, Rufus, on their master jam album.

Released as a trendy 12-inch disc, *Street Player* was one of a number of disco records set on fire and burned during a "death to disco" rally at Comiskey Park, home of the Chicago White Sox. The band may have felt some retribution years later, however, when portions of Street Player were sampled for The Bucketheads smash dance hit, *The Bomb (These Sounds Fall Into My Mind)*, which used the horn, rhythm track, and a bit of Peter Cetera's lead vocal track. Cetera joked about the Bucketheads version on his solo tour, saying that he was oblivious to the song until his hairdresser told him how much the singer on the 1995 dance hit sounded like him!

FEELIN' STRONGER EVERY DAY

With Chicago records being burned in their hometown, Walter Parazaider remembers questioning the place of Chicago on the contemporary music scene. "All of a sudden, we start feeling like, where is our place in the whole scheme of this?" The sales performance of CHICAGO 13 only served to deepen this concern. The album only made it to Number 21 and fell off the charts after only ten weeks, though it went gold in December 1979. According to Parazaider, the album "hit the wall at 700,000" copies, a good sale for some, but very disappointing by Chicago's standards. "We realized that we couldn't show up at the studio and belch on record and have hits," is the way Parazaider puts it.

The direction the band would take was further complicated by the dismissal of Donnie Dacus. According to Robert Lamm, Dacus was fine on a musical level, but "on a personality level, that's where Dacus ran into trouble. It was touring where we learned about that, 'cause that's when you are in the trenches." Peter Cetera agrees. "Once we had Dacus in the group, I think after a tour or so, we started to realize that it was a terrible mistake, because here we were trying to do something else." At the dawn of a new decade, the band's faith in itself was shaken.

CHICAGO XIV

COLUMBIA FC36517

Peter Cetera ～ Laudir de Oliveira ～ Robert Lamm ～ Lee Loughnane ～
James Pankow ～ Walter Parazaider ～ Danny Seraphine ～ Chris Pinnick ～

～

Guest appearances: David "Hawk" Wolinski, Mark Goldenberg, Ian Underwood

Side 1
Manipulation
Upon Arrival
Song For You
Where Did The Lovin' Go
Birthday Boy

Side 2
Hold On
Overnight Cafe
Thunder and Lightning
I'd Rather Be Rich
The American Dream

With CHICAGO 13 and guitarist Donnie Dacus behind them, the members of Chicago once again found themselves starting over. Unlike the comeback the group made from Terry Kath's death and James William Guercio's dismissal, Chicago was now in a very vulnerable position. The CHICAGO 13 album did not fare well and many devoted fans lost faith in the band with the hiring of Dacus as Kath's replacement. Chicago's decision to embrace such a volatile form of music as disco, albeit temporarily, didn't help much, either.

So, with what courage and energy was available at the moment, Chicago pressed on to regroup and record a fourteenth album, this time with veteran rock producer Tom Dowd at the board. Dowd had a track record that went all the way back to the 1940s. He had engineered and produced classic records by jazz greats John Coltrane and Charles Mingus, R&B legends Aretha Franklin and Otis Redding, and rock superstars Eric Clapton, Cream, and Rod Stewart.

But before going into the studio, picking a producer, or deciding on a guitarist, the band and their manager, Jeff Wald, signed a brand new, multi-million dollar record deal with their label, Columbia Records. "We sat in a meeting room at Jeff Wald Productions," says James Pankow, "and the Columbia VIPs were on one side of the table, and Wald and us were on the

FEELIN' STRONGER EVERY DAY

other side of the table, and Wald negotiated a deal that was enormously out of proportion. They said 'okay.' There was no way that we should have made that deal," Lamm concludes. "It created a lot of animosity at the company, and it was the wrong time in our career and in the music business at that point. We knew that, and those guys (the Columbia representatives) and Wald knew that, so I think they got into some weird ego thing, which is not unusual."

1980 was not a good year for Chicago to be releasing a record. The band would have been far better off had they gone on hiatus and waited for a friendlier climate to return. The music had taken a turn towards New Wave and Punk, and although Chicago could attempt to assimilate Disco, there was no way that the band could assimilate these darker genres. Chicago's fourteenth album has come to be known as CHICAGO XIV, but the actual title was "Chicago." The band used the same plain title on their fifth album following the Carnegie Hall live recording to mark a new phase in the band's history. For material, this was the band's weakest offering yet. That, coupled with the stark production, made for a poor recording.

Peter Cetera comments on working with Tom Dowd. "To be perfectly frank, I think we gave Tom more than he could handle, 'cause we were more than we could handle, definitely, and we just beat everybody into the ground at that point." The band chose Tom Dowd over latter day super-producer David Foster, who was eager to work with Chicago, but the vibe was not yet right. "Foster had wanted to do CHICAGO XIV with us," Robert Lamm explains, "and we did talk to David Foster, but when he came to meet us and talk about what we could do, he was a little jive, a little too smooth. Something jarred us or turned us away from him, and we thought; 'Let's go with a warhorse like Tom Dowd.' I guess Tom Dowd was coming off a big Rod Stewart album, so we thought this guy might be hot, rather than taking a chance with a new guy like David Foster." Dowd's production may have been in keeping with the times, but it did not work for Chicago. The band had always thrived on a rich, layered texture, and the techniques used on XIV were too bare-bones, too stark.

Chicago recorded the new album without officially hiring a new guitarist as a band member. Instead, they opted to use Chris Pinnick as a sideman on the record and on the road. "Chris Pinnick came closest to Terry's rhythmic approach," comments Robert Lamm. As Pinnick recalls, "I was hired by Danny Seraphine, whom I had done projects with before Chicago." He counts Terry Kath as one of his early influences. "I listened to him play a lot." While he didn't consciously try to sound like Kath, his playing might remind people of

CHICAGO XIV

Kath because Jimi Hendrix influenced both guitarists. One listen to the first cut on the new record makes you wonder how things may have developed if Chicago had replaced Kath with Pinnick initially. The guitarist brought Chicago back up to the level of musicianship their fans expected from them. The songs, unfortunately, were a different story.

There were no hits. It was as if everyone's muse had gone on vacation at once. Lamm turned in one good, solid tune with the album's opener, *Manipulation*, a heavy-handed rocker that at times bordered on fusion. The song was most memorable for providing a launching pad for Chris Pinnick's outstanding guitar playing. Another Lamm song, *Doin' Business*, had the same power, but was cut from the album. It appeared on the 1991 Group Portrait box set. "I had been listening to some punk bands, and I was trying to see where that fit into what Chicago could do," notes Lamm. "Both *Doin' Business* and *Manipulation* are Chicago's version of what was going on in 1980."

While Lamm was trying to push Chicago into the '80s by exhibiting some angst, Pankow was doing what he could to keep the band's political nature alive. "I wrote a song called *The American Dream*, which lyrically was much better than it was musically," remembers Pankow. "It was taking shots at Capitol Hill, and the general mistrust of government that was pervasive in that day and age."

> Capitol Hill is gonna crumble
> Falling apart at the seams
> We're mighty tired of seeing you stumble
> You're crushing the American Dream . . .
> —James Pankow, *The American Dream* (ASCAP)

Peter Cetera stayed true to his school and wrote a couple of decent rock tunes and a couple of touching ballads. His *Overnight Café* was an honest attempt at blending the newly popularized reggae that bands like The Police were bringing into vogue, with classic rock and the Chicago sound, or at least the Peter Cetera Chicago sound. *Song For You*, one of the two ballads, was a somewhat updated version of Cetera's biggest song, *If You Leave Me Now*. "I love *Song For You*, and I'm actually thinking someday that I'm gonna re-record that," says Cetera. He hasn't to this day, and the version on CHICAGO XIV, released as a single, failed to chart.

The other song released as a single was *Thunder And Lightning*, written by

FEELIN' STRONGER EVERY DAY

Robert Lamm and Danny Seraphine. It peaked at Number 56 on the *Billboard* singles chart. The song had a delightful Earth, Wind & Fire vibe. The album's low point was the Danny Seraphine/David 'Hawk' Wolinski composition, *Birthday Boy*. The song sounded like it would have been best recorded and released by either Wayne Newton or John Davidson, but certainly not Chicago.

There were a few songs on the album that would have benefitted from different production and could have possibly dragged the band onto the charts. Cetera's second ballad, *Where Did The Lovin Go*, Lamm's *Thunder And Lightning*, and the Lamm/Cetera collaboration, *Upon Arrival*, could have breathed some life into the album with some major renovations. Ultimately, the record was awkward and stiff. Released in July 1980, CHICAGO XIV peaked at Number 71, horrendous for a Chicago album — especially catastrophic in light of the new multi-million dollar deal with CBS.

In an on-line interview, fourteen years after the fact, Danny Seraphine shares his thoughts on the whole CHICAGO XIV experience. "You gotta remember, that was a really tough time. Terry died. And so, I'm not making excuses, but you have to understand that when you've got guys in the band that have serious drug problems and alcohol problems. You've got Peter Cetera, who was just about ready to leave the band. He had one foot out of the boat and was ready to go; he just wasn't happy. It was a very, very tough situation. It wasn't Tom Dowd's fault." Any blame aside, Chicago's collective back was against the wall like never before. The failure of CHICAGO XIV, coupled with the enormous contract that CBS was now burdened with, led to the band being dropped by the label. Two years after losing Terry Kath and breaking away from James William Guercio, Chicago was experiencing its darkest days.

CHICAGO XV

GREATEST HITS VOL. 2

COLUMBIA FC 37682

Peter Cetera ∞ Terry Kath ∞ Danny Seraphine ∞ Lee Loughnane ∞ James Pankow ∞ Walter Parazaider ∞ Robert Lamm ∞ Laudir de Oliveira ∞ Donnie Dacus

Side 1
Baby What A Big Surprise
Dialogue (Part II)
No Tell Lover
Alive Again
Old Days

Side 2
If You Leave Me Now
Questions 67 & 68
Happy Man
Gone Long Gone
Take Me Back To Chicago

Despite the fact that CHICAGO XIV "went aluminum, maybe plywood," to use James Pankow's words, Chicago's fifteenth was right on schedule. The 1981 album was the band's official Greatest Hits, Volume 2, and fulfilled Chicago's contractual obligation to Columbia Records who had become disillusioned with the band after the limited success of CHICAGO XIV. CBS "bought us out of the remainder of our contract," says Walt Parazaider. "They gave us a settlement. We gave them the fifteenth album, which was a greatest hits. We took that money and bankrolled the sixteenth album, changed managers, and basically said, 'Let's make the best record we possibly can, and shop it.'" The *Billboard* review of the Greatest Hits package seemed to concur with Columbia's decision: "Chicago isn't what it used to be — it's not even signed to CBS anymore — but this set shows why it was once the hottest American band in the business."

While the band waited for the Columbia contract to expire before working on CHICAGO 16, taking a much needed break from their 12 year, 12 album run, Peter Cetera chose to secure a record deal for himself and record and release his first solo album. Turning to veteran record mogul, Irving Azoff, Cetera inked a deal with Full Moon, Azoff's own label, distributed by Warner Bros. Azoff, along with long-time Chicago affiliate, Howard Kaufman, ran the label and acted as Cetera's management.

FEELIN' STRONGER EVERY DAY

Released in December 1981, the self-titled album was filled mostly with guitar-driven pop/rock. Cetera is listed as writer for all selections and as producer, along with Jim Boyer, who engineered Chicago's twelfth and thirteenth albums. Cetera plays bass on nine of the ten tracks, giving one of the record's best ballads, On The Line, to session great Bob Glaub. Toto's Steve Lukather plays guitar on the single Livin' In The Limelight, which was an instant Rock radio sensation. The song took Cetera as far away from his Chicago association as possible, the direction the artist claimed that he wanted to go in for some time.

Other musicians employed on the album included Chris Pinnick, who played guitar on CHICAGO XIV, Beach Boy Carl Wilson, Ricky Fataar (The Beach Boy's drummer at the time), and guitarist Mark Goldenberg, who had contributed guitar parts to CHICAGO XIV. Goldenberg and Cetera would form a partnership that would yield several memorable tunes, including a future hit for Chicago. During the '80s, Goldenberg was a member of the critically acclaimed L.A. band, The Cretones. He also played guitar and wrote several songs on Linda Ronstadt's highly successful MAD LOVE album, released in 1980, and, while a staff writer for MCA, penned The Pointer Sister's smash hit, Automatic. He also worked with Peter Frampton, Elton John, Jackson Browne, Willie Nelson, Ringo Starr, and Bonnie Raitt, to name a few, and has heard his songs covered by the likes of Olivia Newton-John, Anne Murray, Judy Collins, Selena, Cher, and Natalie Imbruglia.

A fellow Chicagoan, Goldenberg speaks of his association with Peter Cetera. "I met Peter before I ever came to Los Angeles. I was in a band managed by Rick Canoff, one of the ex-members of the Flock, a fairly successful Chicago band; he introduced me to Peter. We met again once I had moved to L.A. Rick took me out to Peter's place. I think Peter became more aware of me after The Cretones became more well known." The Flock, like Chicago and Blood, Sweat & Tears were playing jazz rock in the late 1960s, so well that Stuart Nicholson, in his book *Jazz Rock, A History*, states the debut album by the Flock from 1969 "says more in one disc than Chicago were able to do in XVIII, or BS&T, who spent most of the early 1970s denying that they were over-precise and clinical, in all theirs."

Goldenberg remembers working with Cetera on his solo album. "Peter wanted to do something with more guitars and no horns, more Beatle-like," he notes. "We had been writing and he liked my jangly style, I guess. I remember we had a lot of fun. Peter, who had a lot of experience recording, pretty much

CHICAGO XV

knew what he wanted, but he gave me room to come up with interesting parts." When asked about Cetera's attitude toward Chicago at that point, Goldenberg states, "I think at the time he was fairly down on being in the band. They had been together for so long, I think he needed to stretch out and find his own musical voice."

Aside from the hard rocking *Livin' In The Limelight* and the ballad *On The Line*, Peter Cetera's first offering was what could be expected from the man who wrote such diverse tunes as *Lowdown*, *Where Do We Go From Here*, *In Terms Of Two*, and CHICAGO VIII's *Hideaway*. Several facets of his personality and musicality were explored on songs like the country-fied *Not Afraid To Cry* and *Holy Moly*, as well as the funkier *Mona Mona* and *How Many Times*. The record's most Beatle-like tribute was the song *Practical Man*, which featured Cetera singing through a vocoder, à la ELO's Jeff Lynn, and *Mr. Blue Sky* with a horn part reminiscent of many a Lennon and McCartney tune.

While the album didn't make a solo star out of Peter Cetera, it did give the artist a chance to emancipate himself from the group for a moment. The album remained on the *Billboard* charts for over nine weeks. But more than that, his affiliation and alliance with Azoff and Full Moon would turn out to be extremely important to Chicago during the next phase of their career. In fact, if not for Cetera's relationship with the label, there may not have been a CHICAGO 16.

CHICAGO XVI

FULL MOON/WARNER 23689-1

Robert Lamm ⋙ James Pankow ⋙ Lee Loughnane ⋙ Peter Cetera ⋙ Bill Champlin ⋙ Danny Seraphine ⋙ Walter Parazaider ⋙ David Foster keyboards) ⋙ Steve Lukather, Chris Pinnick, Michael Landau (guitars) ⋙ David Paitch (synthesizer) ⋙ Steve Porcaro (synthesizer programming)

Side 1	Side 2
What You're Missing	Follow Me
Waiting For You To Decide	What Can I Say
Bad Advice	Rescue You
Chains	Love Me Tomorrow
Hard To Say I'm Sorry	
Get Away	

The title of Chicago's sixteenth album should have been 'Born Again'. For a band that was written off by the critics, the radio, the public, and their record label, Chicago came back swinging and landed a knockout punch. As *Billboard* enthused, "Chicago's first album for WEA after a decade with CBS is filled with the distinctive hooks that made it the top American band throughout most of the '70s. The group's cool vocal sound contrasts with the hot, horn-sparked arrangements on a series of tunes ranging from mid-tempo ballads to catchy car-radio rockers. Bill Champlin, formerly of Sons of Champlin, is the group's newest member, replacing Donnie Dacus, who stepped in following the death of Terry Kath in 1978."

Waking the band from its musical coma took a lot of work and faith on behalf of a lot of people, none the least of which was Irving Azoff. Nicknamed the "poison dwarf" for his size and demeanor, Azoff had a tyrannical reputation, but was one of the most successful businessmen in the music industry. In the mid '70s, he started Frontline Management, which eventually managed some of the biggest acts in popular music, including The Eagles, Steely Dan, Boz Scaggs, Heart, Jackson Browne, and, of course, Chicago. Robert Lamm recognizes just how much Irving Azoff's belief in the band helped. "Without him, we wouldn't be here. He gave us a chance when nobody else would."

CHICAGO XVI

The chance that Lamm was speaking of came after Chicago's self-financed sixteenth album had been turned down by all the major record labels.

Since Peter Cetera had already signed a deal for himself with Azoff's label, Full Moon, and his management company, Frontline Management, he and the band reached out to Azoff, who reciprocated with a contract. Howard Kaufman, also a partner in Full Moon and Frontline Management, was an old friend and ally of the band. He continues to manage Chicago today.

The official band line up now included Cetera, Lamm, Parazaider, Seraphine, Loughnane, and Pankow. This streamlined band still needed another member — the gutsy, bluesy, soulful entity that never materialized after Terry Kath passed away. Chicago had always been about the ensemble and a major part was missing. The band finally realized that filling that hole was going to take some serious Spackle, and they found that in one of the most respected singer/songwriter/musicians of all time, Bill Champlin.

Born on May 21, 1947, in Oakland, California, Champlin took up the piano at age three. "I was reading music before I could read English," he states. Like so many of his peers, he began to become enamored with music as a possible path in life after seeing Elvis Presley. "That's when I took up the guitar," he recalls." I took a million music classes in high school and tried to learn as many instruments as I could because I wanted to get a masters degree in music." It was in high school that Bill joined the band, The Opposite Six. "We became the house band at this local community center," he explains, "and we backed up a lot of the acts they brought in, like the Righteous Brothers and Jan and Dean. But our thing was R&B, the James Brown stuff."

The Opposite Six eventually became the Sons of Champlin, the seminal San Francisco band that garnered a huge cult following. The band released its first single on Verve Records in 1965. Champlin was pursuing his music degree at the College of Marin when the band started to get rolling. "My music theory teacher, Larry Snyder, suggested that I drop out because I was doing better music with my band than I was ever going to do in school," Champlin remembers.

The Sons of Champlin went on to release seven albums before breaking up in 1977. With song titles like *Minus Seeds and Stems* and the 7:45 minute long *Get High*, as well as Champlin and guitarist Terry Haggerty's publishing company, Stay High Music, there was, indeed, a theme running through the band's body of work, which could have been dubbed "Pot Rock."

Like Chicago, The Sons utilized horns and percussion, and had an outstanding lead guitarist, whose first name, coincidentally, was Terry. But the

FEELIN' STRONGER EVERY DAY

Sons of Champlin were much more soulful and loose than Chicago. While some of The Sons of Champlin's material bore a resemblance to early Chicago efforts, such as *1982-A* from LOOSEN UP NATURALLY, released in 1969, the band's sound was definitely comprised more of Blues, Gospel, and R&B. When The Sons headed in a more Beatle-ish direction with some of their tunes, the similarities were greater, just like when Chicago showed their blues and R&B side on songs like *South California Purples*, *Vote For Me*, *Skin Tight*, and *What's This World Coming To*. Though The Sons of Champlin emerged from San Francisco in the late '60s, their R&B and Soul elements identified them more with bands like Sly and the Family Stone and Tower of Power than their more psychedelic neighbors, The Jefferson Airplane and The Grateful Dead.

With The Sons behind him (for now), Bill Champlin came to Los Angeles, and, in 1977, began to establish himself as a session player and songwriter. He also began collaborating with the man who would be the next key figure in Chicago's resurrection, producer/arranger/writer David Foster. "The Sons of Champlin did an album that Keith Olsen produced," says Champlin. "It was called A CIRCLE FILLED WITH LOVE (Ariola, 1976) . . . and he thought that some of the songs would be great with a couple of real strings. He said that he knew a piano player who was a good arranger and was looking for work. That was David Foster." Champlin wasn't thrilled with the idea of adding strings to The Sons sound, but he thought, "Why not give it a try?" He met with Foster and they became good friends and established a working relationship.

David Foster was another key figure who was instrumental in reanimating the former supergroup. Some might say that Foster was single-handedly responsible for Chicago's resurrection and imminent return to glory. Foster studied classical music in his native Vancouver before touring England as a keyboardist with Chuck Berry and Fats Domino. In 1973, he came to Los Angeles with his band, Skylark, which had a hit record with the R&B staple, *Wildflower*. The group disbanded shortly thereafter, and Foster quickly established himself as one of the top studio musicians in town. During the mid '70s, he played on albums by Barbara Streisand, Rod Stewart, Dolly Parton, and George Harrison. He also contributed to the soundtrack album for the *Rocky Horror Picture Show*. As a producer, Foster's clients had included, among others, Hall and Oates, and The Average White Band.

Champlin and Foster first worked together on a record for singer and Gong Show regular, J.P. Morgan. The album also featured the talents of Kenny Loggins and Ray Parker, Jr. The album never got released. Foster's second credit

CHICAGO XVI

as producer was with "a couple of kids named the Keane Brothers," he recalls. "We had one single that came on the charts at 90 and fell off with an anchor." The saying goes, "The third time's a charm," and in David Foster's case, that was true. His next project was Bill Champlin's first solo album, 1978's SINGLE, for CBS Records. The album featured songs written by Champlin and Foster, and was recorded by a veritable who's-who of L.A. studio elite. SINGLE was Bill Champlin at his best. His wide ranged, emotional vocals were showcased to perfection. The material was both sophisticated and accessible. His compositions with David Foster, *We Both Tried* and *Keys To The Kingdom*, were beautifully executed, harbingers of the style and sound that these two men would bring to the new Chicago.

The record was a very good companion piece to Boz Scaggs' 1977 CBS release, DOWN TWO THEN LEFT, no small coincidence, since both artists employed the talents of David Foster's favorite session musicians, guitarist Steve Lukather, drummer Jeff Porcaro, bassist David Hungate, and keyboardist David Paitch, though Paitch did not play on this particular Boz Scaggs record. These session musicians later formed TOTO, one of the most popular pop bands of the late '70s and early '80s.

Another curious feature of Bill Champlin's album SINGLE was the fact that the album was recorded on Azoff and Kaufman's Full Moon label, which, at the time, was being distributed by Epic Records/CBS. All things considered, it seemed inevitable that Bill Champlin, if not both he and David Foster, would end up working with Chicago.

According to David Foster, working with Champlin on this record was a big break. "Bill Champlin," he states, "led to my work with Earth, Wind & Fire." Champlin, Foster, and writer/guitarist Jay Graydon co-wrote the song *After The Love Is Gone*, which became a tremendous hit for Earth, Wind & Fire from their 1979 LP, I AM. Foster co-wrote, arranged, and played on six tunes on this double-platinum album. *After The Love Is Gone* garnered the 1979 Grammy Award for Best Rhythm and Blues Song. As EW&F's Verdine White recalls, "I AM was like our ABBEY ROAD. It really scored pop." The producer of the album, Maurice White, remarks, "I think of it as a milestone album. People stole stuff from that album, whole careers came out of it. It was like . . . listen to I AM and see what you can steal. All the pieces came together."

In 1981, David Foster went back in the studio with Bill Champlin to produce the singer's second solo disc, RUNAWAY, this time for Elektra Records. Like SINGLE, RUNAWAY was filled with beautiful ballads, funky groove tunes, and

FEELIN' STRONGER EVERY DAY

the best musicians and singers in Los Angeles. This time around, Kenny Loggins' vocals were added to the mix. While the album has been critically acclaimed and highly regarded by fans, Champlin's not convinced. "Both David and I thought that SINGLE was a much, much, much better album than RUNAWAY."

While RUNAWAY was still fresh, but not going very far, Bill Champlin was helping Danny Seraphine steer Chicago to its next destination. Champlin and Seraphine had worked together in the late '70s. "Danny was producing an album for a guy named Angelo," recounts Champlin, "and he called me and asked me to do some background vocals. It just so happened that Peter Cetera was also singing. Peter and I had a lot of fun together and became friends. We did all the background vocals for Angelo's albums for some years."

Later on, Seraphine turned to Champlin for his writing skills. "Danny Seraphine and I had written a song called *Sonny Think Twice*," Champlin explains. "Danny was putting together material for a new Chicago album at the time. He also mentioned that they needed a new producer. He called me and asked me if I thought that David Foster would be good for them. I said, 'You'll probably end up rewriting a lot, but I think Foster would be great for you guys.'"

The next phone call Champlin received was also from Seraphine, only this time asking him to work with Chicago. "Danny called and said they wanted me to play with the band," he remembers. "I knew that Chicago was using sidemen, and I said to Danny that I didn't want to be a sideman, because RUNAWAY was just released." Champlin felt that it would be a conflict of interest to tour with a band as a hired hand at that point. "Danny's response was that the job was not for a sideman . . . he wanted me to be a band member. I asked him if I could think about it for a while, and when I realized that Elektra wasn't giving RUNAWAY any support, I said yes to Chicago."

With Champlin and Foster in place, the new Chicago was ready to orchestrate what *BAM* (Bay Area Music) magazine called the "Biggest Comeback of the Year (1982)." CHICAGO 16 brought the band back into the arms — or the hands, however you want to look at it — of a strong producer. With David Foster, Chicago not only found themselves sharing the writing with him, but for the first time, with the exception of Chicago Transit Authority's *I'm A Man*, the band was covering songs by outside writers. While the members of the band may have had a problem with giving up control and so quickly losing their freedom from the likes of Guercio, the end result was tremendous.

CHICAGO XVI

Chicago had started out as a band full of formidable talent that was shaped by an experienced record maker, James Guercio, and the phenomenal success that they achieved under his rule was undeniable. In retrospect, it was when the band took their career into their own hands that things started to go awry. There is no shame or failure in letting those who can, do. And David Foster was definitely someone who could, and did, restore Chicago to superstar status. Chicago's work with David Foster yielded some of their best work ever. The producer brought back a key element to the band's sound: sophistication. His classical training and approach to harmony and arrangements fit the band like a glove.

David Foster speaks of his initial contact with Chicago. "When they first came out around 1967," he remembers, "I just fell in love with their music. So when the opportunity presented itself. . . . I went to one of those big boardroom-type meetings and they all showed up. In the end, they, or the record company, CBS, at that time, decided I wasn't the right guy. I was crushed. So then they went on and made CHICAGO XIV, which I think was not a good album at all; there was not a hit within 25 miles of that LP." Foster feels that when it came time to hire a producer for the 16th album, he was considered because of his acquired experience. "When it came time for that album," he explains, "I think the drummer, Danny Seraphine, kind of reached out and thought that I might now be the right guy since I'd had a couple more years experience under my belt. So I went to a meeting and they started playing the tunes for 16 and I remember being very impressed with their musicianship, but not impressed with the songs. So, at that point, I made a commitment where I would go to their homes and work until we had what I thought were ten acceptable songs. We ended up writing fifteen songs, of which I was co-writer on about nine of them." Foster actually co-wrote eight of the ten tunes that ended up on CHICAGO 16. Three songs, *What You're Missing*, *Chains*, and *Waiting For You To Decide*, were penned by writers outside of the band.

With all of the changes that took place within the organization, both musical and structural, the Chicago sound was not that drastically different. It was, instead, a refined, modernized return to all the qualities that made Chicago appealing in the first place. "It was really simple," says David Foster of how he went about dialing in the new Chicago sound. "I just tried to be like them. I tried to imitate what I loved about them — the trombones, the good melodies with Peter Cetera singing high and tight, and the double vocals. I just thought they had gotten off the track and I tried to make them sound like they used

> **FEELIN' STRONGER EVERY DAY**

to sound. I obviously applied my own musicianship and that came up with what we would call the new Chicago sound. Maybe not terribly innovative, but certainly commercial."

And "commercial" was the key. It was evident that the band had grown beyond their youthful musical ideals of not wanting to be a 'single's band' and now realized that in order to stay alive in the music industry, and to maintain the degree of success that they were used to, they needed hit songs. CHICAGO 16 took them all the way back to Number 1.

Released in June 1982, CHICAGO 16 entered the *Billboard* album charts at Number 75. The magazine also contained a full-page ad for the album on the front inside cover. Radio, at least in Los Angeles, promoted the album heavily, and there was an unusual amount of press and visibility for the band. *People Magazine* praised the album in it's "picks and pans" section, saying that Chicago must have been taking vitamins! By September, CHICAGO 16 rose all the way to Number 9 and stayed there for four weeks. The album's first single, *Hard To Say I'm Sorry*, a tune that would serve as the blueprint for Chicago's new formula for success, reached Number 1.

> Hold me now
> It's hard for me to say I'm sorry
> I just want you to stay
> After all that we've been through
> I will make it up to you
> I promise to
> And after all that's been said and done
> You're just part of me I can't let go
> — Peter Cetera/David Foster, *Hard To Say I'm Sorry* (ASCAP)

Hard To Say I'm Sorry was used in the soundtrack for the movie *Summer Lovers*. After the breezy successes of *Grease* and *The Blue Lagoon*, director Randall Kleiser made *Summer Lovers*, which involved a love triangle between Daryl Hannah, Peter Gallagher, and French actress Valérie Quennessen. The film was a sensuous ménage à trois, accompanied by a soundtrack full of early-'80s pop by Chicago, Elton John, Blondie, The Pointer Sisters, and others. The triumphant return to the Top Ten on the *Billboard* charts was a true testament of Chicago's tenacity, Foster's brilliance, and the loyalty of their fans.

Hard To Say I'm Sorry, written by Peter Cetera and David Foster, featured

CHICAGO XVI

Cetera singing at the top of his game, plus an impressive guitar solo by Chris Pinnick, who was fortunate enough to have survived CHICAGO XIV and be involved with the new regime. The song ended with a piano part reminiscent of Earth, Wind & Fire's *After The Love Is Gone* (no surprise) and segued into the wildly frenetic *Get Away*, written by Cetera, Foster, and Robert Lamm. *Get Away* was the new Chicago at full throttle, but it was the only piece of music on CHICAGO 16 to be written, even in part, by Robert Lamm.

Lamm admits that this was not a very easy time for him. "I don't want to get specific," he says, "but my life was a shambles." It was during this period in time that the usually prolific singer and songwriter was going through a painful second divorce. He admits that this situation kept him "too distracted" to do much writing for the album. He also admits that he had a slight problem with the addition of Bill Champlin to the band, but only briefly. "My ego was saying, 'What the hell is this? I'm a keyboard player. Why do we need another one?' The fact is," he concedes, "that he's a better player than me, and he plays guitar, too. He's good for the band." Lamm also realizes that Champlin's vocal abilities cannot be denied. "We needed that kind of voice. Nobody else in the band could sing in that range; it's that gruff, soul style. With Bill in the band, there are a lot of songs we can do that we stopped doing when Terry died."

CHICAGO 16, forever after, associated the band with the 'power ballad', a term that would be used to describe many successful hits of the '80s. It was the marriage of big, distorted guitars, huge-sounding drums, and Neil Diamond-style ballads. Chicago happened to be at the forefront, and Peter Cetera and David Foster took the genre to its apogee. A fine example of the new sound was the second single, *Love Me Tomorrow*, also written by Cetera and Foster. The song reached Number 22 on the *Billboard* Singles chart. Big drums, silky keyboards, powerful guitars, emotional vocals, a strong hook, and lush orchestration all made this song a radio mainstay.

The rest of CHICAGO 16 was comprised of well crafted pop rock pleasantries that all made sense. There wasn't a dud in the bunch. While Foster and the new label made sure to keep the focus on Peter Cetera, Bill Champlin did have his turn. The seasoned singer created duets with Cetera on the soulful *Bad Advice*, written by Cetera, James Pankow, and David Foster. He also sang lead on Pankow/Foster's *Follow Me* and sounded most at home on the tune that brought him together with the band in the first place, *Sonny Think Twice*, his previously mentioned collaboration with Danny Seraphine. His contributions to the background vocal arrangements enhanced the band's sound and overall vocal infrastructure.

With all the welcome additions to the band for CHICAGO 16, a couple of things were missing. Laudir de Oliveira was no longer with the band. Whether the percussionist had grown tired and wanted to move on, or the new Chicago no longer required his services, was unclear. All attempts to find out what he did after leaving Chicago came up negative. Whatever the case may have been, he did share in the band's rich history, and it was sad to see him go without fanfare.

Also missing from the new sound was Peter Cetera's bass. Although he still played on all the tunes from the record in concert, the one-time bass legend put the instrument on the stand and let the synthesizers handle the low end for a portion of CHICAGO 16. His electric bass all but disappeared by the following album. Of Peter's seeming loss of interest in the bass, Bob Ludwig offers this explanation. "In the '80s, Peter would tend to just hold the bass and he would be working his voice. It got to the point where Lee would start playing bass notes on a Moog because Peter just wanted to sing. He gradually started playing less and less bass, putting it to the side. His vocals were superb. He was definitely becoming the front man in the band, but we were really lacking live in the bass. That's probably why Foster gave him the support on record. He was promoting his vocals more. But in the early days, Peter was a phenomenal bass player. I would sit behind his huge SVT amps on stage, and listen to him and Danny and think, 'Man . . . this is incredible! Who else is doing that?'"

Some of the same crew of studio musicians present for Bill Champlin's album, produced by David Foster, were on hand for CHICAGO 16. "They say that I function best when I have my ringers around me," Foster acknowledges. In addition to Chris Pinnick and Bill Champlin, guitarists Steve Lukather and Michael Landau were present, with Lukather and Foster co-writing one of the songs, *Waiting For You To Decide*, and TOTO band mate, David Paitch. The new Chicago music and Foster's arrangements called for more and demanding keyboard parts than ever before. Four different keyboard players worked on CHICAGO 16. David Foster and David Paitch, who was credited for synthesizer programming, joined Robert Lamm and Bill Champlin. For the live shows, Lamm and Champlin covered most of the parts, with James Pankow and Lee Loughnane doubling occasionally. While this may have been out of the ordinary for Chicago, it was in keeping with the times, as music in the '80s seemed to be dominated by keyboards and synthesizers. Consequently, the tour

CHICAGO XVI

for CHICAGO 16 was called "The MIDI tour," and the album cover and jacket showed the Chicago logo plugged into a circuit board, not-so-subtle hints that the band was given an overhaul for the new decade.

When Chicago hit the road to support the album, they had gained a tremendous new following that caught them by surprise. "We had a big resurgence then," says Walter Parazaider. "I had a kid come up to me and say, 'I have your first record, would you mind signing it?' This was somewhere in North Carolina. We were going on stage, and I told her I would sign it after the show. And what she had was the CHICAGO 16 album. She had no idea about the others that came before it. The reality hit, we had gained another generation [of fans]."

Live, the new band was unbeatable. Chris Pinnick and Bill Champlin both turned out guitar solos that undoubtedly brought back many fans who had left the band when Kath died. The vocals were stunning, rounded out by Champlin's new take on classics like *Make Me Smile* and *Colour My World* (although he would eventually stop singing the latter song because of his lack of commitment to the original melody). With Champlin on board, the scope of the songs and the arrangements became broader, as did the vocal harmonies. Where complacency had crept in during recent years, the current tour was exciting and intense. To the fans, Chicago was once again a supergroup to be enjoyed on record and in concert. To skeptics, whether or not the band's comeback was a fluke, remained to be seen. In January 1983, *What You're Missing* was released as the third single from CHICAGO 16. The song only reached Number 81, but that didn't matter. Chicago's next album would produce four hit singles and become their biggest-selling album to date.

CHICAGO XVII

WARNER BROS./FULL MOON 25060

Danny Seraphine (drums) ∞ Peter Cetera (bass and vocals) ∞ Bobby Lamm (keyboards and vocals) ∞ Bill Champlin (guitar and vocals) ∞ Jimmy Pankow (trombone) ∞ Chris Pinnick (guitar) ∞ Walter Parazaider (woodwinds) ∞ Lee Loughnane (trumpet) ∞ Michael Landau, Paul Jackson, Mark Goldenberg (guitar) ∞ Paulinho da Costa (percussion) ∞ David Foster, John van Tongeren, Erich Bulling, Marcus Ryle (synthesizer programming) ∞ Garry Grant, Greg Adams (horns) ∞ Ken Cetera, Donny Osmond, Richard Marx (background vocals)

Side 1
Stay The Night
We Can Stop The Hurtin'
Hard Habit To Break
Only You
Remember The Feeling

Side 2
Along Comes A Woman
You're The Inspiration
Please Hold On
Prima Donna
Once In A Lifetime

Released in May 1984, CHICAGO 17 broke all records for a Chicago studio album. The new album went through the roof with sales in excess of 7 million copies. CHICAGO 17 entered the charts at Number 91 on June 2, 1984, and ended up at Number 4 by February 2, 1985, a long-lived run. "We had a great time playing the big time again," states Lee Loughnane. "It was the second big wave. People would give their eyeteeth for the first amount of success that we had in the '70s. To be able to do it for a second time is a major milestone in the history of rock and roll, as well as Chicago's history. Not many people have had this opportunity, and we had a lot of fun with it." The album was also a critical success for reasons indicated in the *Billboard* review: "Clearly emboldened by their platinum comeback with '16', the veteran pop/rock band doesn't just go by the numbers here. If smooth ballads helped lay an AC and pop base last time around, the new set gives crucial weight to tougher, more aggressive songs (like the first single, 'Stay The Night') edged with new music accents and dance-oriented production effects. Those core audiences are still well served here, with glossy, harmonized love songs like 'Hard Habit To Break,' while producer Foster's blueprint again embellishes the band's signature brass voicing with lush electronic keyboards. In short a multi-format crossover contender."

Once again, David Foster was the man in charge. He speaks out on making records with Chicago. "With Chicago, there are seven really strong individuals. To say that it went absolutely smoothly would be a gross overstatement. But out of that conflict comes greatness, sometimes." This time, like the first effort, was no exception. "With Chicago, I'm talking seven co-producers, and that's where the problem comes in. That's difficult. On the one hand, who am I to tell Chicago how to play something? I mean, I was just a fan of theirs. They've had more success than I might ever have. On the other hand, we've got this great run going for which I'm largely responsible. That's why it's so difficult to make records together, and at some point you just say, 'Ah, shit, I don't want to do this again,' and I'm sure they don't. We're enjoying the success and the money, but it took six months of hard work for CHICAGO 17 and over a year to do 16."

The hard work paid off. CHICAGO 17 was a masterpiece. This time around, David Foster co-wrote only four of the ten songs but took arranging credit for eight. The album was chock full of guest artists and session musicians. Donny Osmond and Richard Marx added background vocals along with Peter Cetera's brother, Kenny, who went on the CHICAGO 17 tour with the band as a singer and percussionist. Lionel Richie even made a contribution as co-writer on the song *Please Hold On*, along with Bill Champlin and David Foster. Guitarist and songwriter Mark Goldenberg was back collaborating with Peter Cetera. The pair wrote two songs, *Prima Donna* and *Along Comes A Woman*. *Prima Donna* also appeared on the soundtrack to the Olivia Newton-John movie, *Two Of A Kind*, and *Along Comes A Woman*, which was the fourth hit single from the album, charted at Number 14. The track was re-mixed from the album by Foster and his engineer, Humberto Gatica. Gatica remembers the circumstances. "Being able to update your sound and change is the only way you can last in this business. What sounded good yesterday won't sound good today. Music changes so drastically." This was especially true in the early '80s, when everything from the '70s was deemed tragically unhip. "We put the album [CHICAGO 17] out a year-and-a-half before the single *Along Comes A Woman* was released," he explains. "If we hadn't done the remix, I think the song would have struggled and gotten lost between the twenties and

FEELIN' STRONGER EVERY DAY

thirties [on the charts]. We changed the feel [of the song] because David was very unhappy with the bass part of it. I had never liked the feel of the original mix. The drums were stiff, so we put on new drums and fixed the song up. It ended up being a big hit."

Mark Goldenberg remembers working with David Foster on the record. "David was cool. He seemed to produce with a firm hand. He knew what he wanted to hear." As for all the co-producers being in the studio at one time, Goldenberg claims that wasn't what he saw. "When I over dubbed [my guitar parts], it was David, Peter and me." He had one word to say about Chicago's new sound, with Bill Champlin and David Foster, "Nice."

Once again, Robert Lamm only had one song on the new album, albeit a good one. Written with Bill Champlin and D. Neal, *We Can Stop The Hurtin'* was a song about the plight of the homeless and downtrodden. At least Lamm was still keeping the band's political conscience alive.

The first single, *Stay the Night*, was a nice coup for the band and the lead singer, Peter Cetera, who wrote the song with Foster. Chicago had actually managed to get a rock tune on the radio and on the charts. The song reached Number 16 and introduced the band to yet another new audience who had probably written them off as a ballad band. "Prior to *Stay The Night*," says Cetera, "we were under the assumption that it was the same audience that has kind of grown up with us, and that very few of the albums were being sold to younger people. After *Stay The Night*, we found out that it's almost the opposite. We still have a lot of old fans, but I think most of our fans now are the younger kids." Although *Stay the Night* broke the power-ballad mold set by *If You Leave Me Now*, the change was short-lived.

The second single, *Hard Habit To Break*, was indeed a ballad, and it went all the way to Number 3. Written by Steve Kipner and J. Parker, the song contained a beautiful duet sung by Peter Cetera and Bill Champlin. Jeremy Lubbock and David Foster shared a Grammy Award that year (1984) for Best Instrumental /Accompanying Vocals for *Hard Habit To Break*, and Humberto Gatica received a Grammy for Best Engineered Recording.

> Now being without you takes a lot of getting used to
> Should learn to live with it
> But I don't want to
> Living without you is all a big mistake
> Instead of getting easier

CHICAGO XVII

> It's the hardest thing to take
> I'm addicted to ya, babe
> You're a hard habit to break . . .
> — Steve Kipner/J. Parker, *Hard Habit To Break* (ASCAP)

The third single from CHICAGO 17, *You're The Inspiration*, has become one of the band's most memorable songs. Written by Cetera and Foster, the song reached Number 3, but unlike *Hard Habit To Break*, it has become a perennial favorite on radio.

> You're the meaning in my life
> You're the inspiration
> You bring feeling to my life
> You're the inspiration
> Wanna have you near me
> I wanna have you hear me sayin'
> No one needs you more than I need you . . .
> — Peter Cetera/David Foster, *You're The Inspiration* (ASCAP)

The album also introduced Chicago to the MTV generation. Although a video was produced for 16's *Love Me Tomorrow*, it was nothing more than the band lip-synching on a sound stage. For CHICAGO 17, all four singles were made into videos. *Stay the Night* featured Peter Cetera pining for a woman who would try to kill him with her car, which winds up crashing through a billboard for the album before exploding. The video featured all the other band members in various supporting roles. The videos for *Hard Habit To Break* and *You're The Inspiration* were filled with typical love song imagery. *Along Comes A Woman* was part Indiana Jones and part *Casablanca*. Cetera was once again the star, with the rest of Chicago relegated to being the house band at the nightclub where the hero spent some of his time when he wasn't being chased through the jungle.

With the increased visibility of the videos, the band was selling out concerts night after night. For the CHICAGO 17 tour, there were nine people on stage. Peter's younger brother, Kenny, added his voice to the mix and played percussion when necessary. The band pulled out more keyboard equipment for this tour, and Pankow and Loughnane doubled more frequently, since some of the recent hits, like *Stay The Night* and *You're The Inspiration*, did not contain

FEELIN' STRONGER EVERY DAY

horns, but did involve orchestration and multiple piano and synthesizer tracks.

With the major personal and professional success of CHICAGO 16 and 17, it appeared that the band had put their problems of the late 1970s and early 1980s behind them. Then came the announcement that after eighteen years, Peter Cetera was no longer a member of Chicago. "After eighteen years, Peter Cetera is no longer the inspiration for Chicago." That is how *Entertainment Tonight* reported the story of Peter Cetera's departure from Chicago in July 1985. Many expected the follow-up piece to be on the breakup of the band, but that piece has never been written.

Cetera claims that the band "Gave me my walking papers." The singer wanted to take a break after all the hard work he and the band had put in over the last couple of albums. He wanted a rest from the studio and the road. David Foster had already told *Modern Recording* magazine in the July issue, which probably came out in June, a month before the official announcement of Cetera's departure, that the singer might not be back for the follow-up to CHICAGO 17. "Yeah, we've been talking about it," Foster comments when asked about the possibility of producing the eighteenth album. "I had made a decision that I didn't want to do it on a personal level of not wanting to go through another six months of really hard work. I felt that we had peaked. But now I feel like there's one more great album between us that's going to have to be made. Peter Cetera really wants to do another solo album, so the decision on CHICAGO 18 rests largely with him. If he does the next album, I'll do the next album." Cetera did not get involved with the making of CHICAGO 18, but David Foster remained with the band, anyway.

"I had always wanted to do the solo thing," says Cetera, "and then after the first album, Chicago kinda promised me that I could do the solo thing, and then they sort of reneged on it, and never gave me the opportunity to do it. They wanted to go one way, and I wanted to go another way, so we decided on a mutual parting. I did not, in fact, quit the group. If anything, I was fired for not going along with what they wanted to do." Cetera proposed to the band that he split his time between Chicago and a solo career. "I wanted to be Phil Collins and Genesis," he says, speaking of the dual career led by the former Genesis frontman, which led to hits for both parties, "but they didn't want any part of that."

Cetera, became, by default, identified as the lead singer of Chicago. "Peter never wanted to be the frontman," states Bob Ludwig. "He used to stutter, he was shy, and he's not the kind of guy who was out there seeking his own

CHICAGO XVII

personal glory. He was more of a group personality. I think he kinda got pushed to the front by David Foster." When Chicago re-tooled for 16, Cetera had in fact become the frontman . . . literally. The band's new stage setup put the singing bassist dead center and left no doubt that he was the lead singer and focal point of Chicago. He was, after all, contributing the bulk of the hit material at the time.

"The group went through three phases," says Cetera. "In the beginning, Bobby Lamm and Terry Kath were the strongest members, in the middle, Jimmy Pankow dominated, and toward the end, I did." Cetera states that the band was not taking his rise to personal glory too well. "They were getting jealous, and I said, 'Well, come on, if you're jealous, then start doing something about it,' but they weren't in the frame of mind to write songs, and I was the one who was in the studio most of the time."

A common misconception was that Terry Kath had been put off by Cetera's success and the direction that the band was heading in after *If You Leave Me Now*. Bob Ludwig offers a different perspective. "Terry and Peter were like brothers, and Terry was very happy for Peter. What made him upset is that he wasn't the one coming up with the ideas anymore. Terry was always leading the charge for Chicago in the early days, and he felt very frustrated that he couldn't come up with anything anymore. Peter was coming up with ideas and it wasn't what Terry wanted to do, but he didn't have any bad feelings toward Peter."

In typical Chicago fashion, the band did not say very much about Cetera's departure. They simply stuck to Loughnane's original statement: "The guy was unhappy, and it's better to have the guy leave than stay and be miserable."

Cetera, after leaving Chicago in 1985, chose not to play live for many years. He finally embarked on a small tour in 1995. His backup band included keyboardist/vocalist Kiki Ebsen, who, curiously enough, worked with Chicago on their first post-Cetera tour and their subsequent nineteenth album and tour. Cetera went on to achieve a great deal of success as a solo artist. In June 1986, he released SOLITUDE/SOLITAIRE. Produced by Michael Omartian for Warner Bros. Records, the album provided him with two Number One singles, *Glory Of Love*, written with David Foster and Diane Nini, and *The Next Time I Fall*, written by Bobby Caldwell. *Glory Of Love* was the featured love theme from the hit movie *Karate Kid, Part II*, and *The Next Time I Fall* was a duet with Amy Grant. At the time, Grant was only known in religious music circles, but

FEELIN' STRONGER EVERY DAY

since her pairing with Cetera, she has become a major star.

Though he has never been able to shake his association with ballads — or Chicago, for that matter — Peter Cetera continues to have a successful recording career. Since SOLITUDE/SOLITAIRE he has released four more solo albums, including one greatest hits package containing some remarkably well crafted remakes of his Chicago hits. He has continued to have a fruitful relationship with David Foster, which included collaboration in 1991 on a project called "Voices That Care," a star-studded benefit project to rally the troops during the Gulf War. Cetera co-wrote the theme song with Foster and shared vocals with the star-studded chorus, which included Celine Dion and The Pointer Sisters. The entire performance, including behind-the-scenes footage of Cetera in the recording studio, is available on video.

After *Glory Of Love* and *The Next Time I Fall*, his string of hits included *One Good Woman* (from the 1988 album ONE MORE STORY, which also contained the song *Save Me*, featuring guitar work by Bonnie Raitt, and was used as the theme song for the first season of *Baywatch*), *Restless Heart, Feels Like Heaven* (both from the 1992 album WORLD FALLING DOWN), and *I Wanna Take Forever Tonight* (from the 1995 album ONE CLEAR VOICE). He also produced an album in 1988 for Agnetha Faltskog of ABBA, which yielded the single *I Wasn't The One (Who Said Goodbye)*. Cetera also had a minor hit from his... A COLLECTION album with a song written by Liz Hengber and Will Robinson called *Do You Love Me That Much*. Many of his recent recordings have fared very well on *Billboard*'s Adult Contemporary Charts. His 1997 remake of his Chicago song *You're The Inspiration* on his album PETER CETERA... YOU'RE THE INSPIRATION... A COLLECTION was also a hit. The song featured background vocals by the R&B vocal group, Az Yet, who that same year had covered the Cetera/Foster hit, *Hard To Say I'm Sorry*, which included Cetera singing a line on the bridge. His work with Az Yet, and the fact that his voice was sampled for The Bucketheads dance hit, *The Bomb (These Sounds Fall Into My Mind)*, as previously mentioned, has helped to keep Peter Cetera current and vital as an artist.

Two of the last pieces of music that Peter Cetera contributed to Chicago before leaving where a 1985 Michelob Light beer jingle, and a track on the historic WE ARE THE WORLD album. The beer commercial jingle was a hybrid musical collage of *Stay The Night, You're The Inspiration*, and other Chicago hits. Cetera and Bill Champlin shared the vocals. The WE ARE THE WORLD song, titled *Good For Nothing*, was written by Robert Lamm, Richard Marx, and

CHICAGO XVII

David Foster. Produced and mixed by Foster and Humberto Gatica, the track sounded like an outtake from the CHICAGO 17 sessions. Cetera provides vocals along with Lamm and is credited for playing bass, although it sounds like his track may have been replaced with a synthesizer.

With Cetera out on his own, Chicago began their search for a replacement. Twenty-three-year old Jason Scheff became the band's new lead singer and bassist. Chicago then set out to prove that nothing or no one could stop them from moving forward. The results of their campaign to stay on top came in the form of CHICAGO 18, released in 1986.

CHICAGO XVIII

WARNER BROS. 25509-1

Bill Champlin (keyboards and vocals) ∞ Robert Lamm (keyboards and vocals) ∞ Lee Loughnane (trumpet) ∞ James Pankow (trombone) ∞ Walter Parazaider (woodwinds) ∞ Jason Scheff (bass and vocals) ∞ Danny Seraphine (drums) ∞ David Foster (keyboards) ∞ Michael Landau, Buzz Feiten, Steve Lukather (guitar) ∞ David Boruff, Michael Boddicker, Rhett Lawrence, Bo Tomlyn (synthesizer programming)

Side 1
Niagara Falls
Forever
If She Would Have Been Faithful
25 Or 6 To 4
Will You Still Love Me?

Side 2
Over And Over
It's Alright
Nothin's Gonna Stop Us Now
I Believe
One More Day

For Chicago's five remaining original members, the idea of calling it quits after losing Peter Cetera was definitely not an option. Instead of cooling their heels and enjoying some well deserved time off after the overwhelming success of CHICAGO 17, the band immediately set out to find a replacement for the man who, in recent years, had become the dominant member of the group. "Mickey Thomas was considered," says Bill Champlin, "and so was Mr. Mister bassist, vocalist, Richard Page." Thomas was the frontman for the venerable rock group, Jefferson Starship, and Richard Page, besides working with Mr. Mister, was a session singer with enormous credits, including Bill Champlin's album RUNAWAY. Page, who's also a fine bass player, "would have been perfect," according to Champlin, "but he didn't want to give up Mr. Mister for Chicago." Not hard to understand since 1985 was the year that Mr. Mister released their second album, WELCOME TO THE REAL WORLD, which gave the band three major hits with *Broken Wings*, *Kyrie*, and *Is It Love*. Page has since said that he turned down Chicago to spend more time with his family. Perhaps he had the foresight to see that Chicago would be one of the longest running acts

CHICAGO XVIII

in the history of popular music and that he would be spending most of his time with them.

The search for Cetera's successor ended with a relatively unknown singing bassist named Jason Scheff. Born in San Diego, California in 1962, Jason Scheff is the son of legendary bassist Jerry Scheff, who toured and recorded with the two Elvises, Presley and Costello, as well as The Doors, among countless others. Jason was playing in local Top 40 bands and starting to carve out a career as a session bassist and singer when he got the break of a lifetime. "I had just signed a publishing deal and I had three songs in the catalog," Scheff explains. "When Peter Cetera left Chicago, he stayed with Warner Bros. Records. I had been signed with the publisher for two months when they got a call asking if they had songs for Peter Cetera's solo album and/or someone to write with him. My publisher said, 'Yeah, as a matter of fact, we have this new kid. We'll send you his stuff.' The next day we get a call from [A&R rep] Michael Ostin's secretary who asked who was singing the songs on the tape. My publisher said, 'It's Jason, the writer.' Since Chicago and Cetera were both with Warner Bros., Michael Ostin heard my tape and said, 'I think we've found the new lead singer for Chicago!'"

Scheff got a call a week later from Howard Kaufman, who arranged a meeting with the young musician. "I went in and he told me that the guys wanted me to be in the band," Scheff recalls. "All I had to do was go audition and take the gig. They didn't even know I was a bass player. Howard Kaufman asked me, 'What instrument do you play?' I said, 'I'm a bass player,' and he freaked out! He said, 'Oh my God! This sounds like a match made in heaven!'"

Scheff auditioned for the band, and when it was all over, he was the new lead singer and bassist for Chicago. He played and sang through some of the newer material, but when the band asked him if there was anything that he would like to play, he said, "How about, *Just You 'N Me?*" His familiarity and affinity for the tune may have sealed the deal for him. With Scheff on board, Chicago was once again whole and ready to tackle yet another phase of their ever-evolving career. The *Billboard* review heralding the new album stated, "Yes, there is life after Cetera."

Despite his comments to the contrary, David Foster was back at the controls for Chicago's eighteenth album. His challenge, this time, was to not only keep the band's momentum going and continue turning out hits, but to make sure that the loss of Peter Cetera could be overcome by

FEELIN' STRONGER EVERY DAY

Jason Scheff . . . at least on record. Foster had his usual team of studio aces on hand, this time aided by guitar great, Buzz Feiten, who co-wrote one the album's best cut with Jason Scheff, *Nothin's Gonna Stop Us Now*.

> He was lost, uncertain
> Only she could see he was waiting for the night to end
> And with just one kiss brought him back into the light again
> He said nothin's gonna stop us now
> He said, baby, nothin's gonna stop us now . . .
> — Jason Scheff/Buzz Feiten, *Nothin's Goona Stop Us Now* (ASCAP)

One person missing from the lineup was guitarist Chris Pinnick. "Chris Pinnick, in my opinion, was Terry Kath reincarnated," offers Bob Ludwig. "He was the only guitar player the band has had that could hold a candle to Terry. He was the nicest guy. He was amazing, and he even looked like Terry!" Peter Cetera echoed Bob's sentiments almost verbatim. The two men agreed that because of Pinnick's image, Chicago relegated him to being the 'guy in the back'. "You couldn't even see Chris unless he was taking a solo," says Ludwig. "And whenever the band took any pictures they would leave him out because he was heavy, and I think that really bothered him." Pinnick suffered a heart attack on his way to a gig in 1996. "Chris had a heart transplant and lost a hundred pounds," says Ludwig, who had the chance to work with a reunited Chicago and Pinnick over the summer in 1999. "It was the first time I'd worked with both parties in over ten years," he says. "Chris sounded awesome. You could see the looks on the guys' faces as he played. It wasn't the whole band, just Lee, Tris, Jason, Bill, and Robert. I don't recall who was filling in for Pankow, but Marty Grebb played sax. He had worked with the band several times, especially right after they got rid of Donnie Dacus. Marty played keys and sax and sang background vocals on some isolated dates that we did for the fourteenth album, which was a bad record. It was Chicago's 'black album.' The Beatles had the WHITE ALBUM, Chicago had XIV, the black album!" Marty Grebb was a member of the Buckinghams back in 1968, which most likely led to his association with Chicago.

One good thing that happened was the re-emergence of Robert Lamm. The troubled singer/songwriter seemed to be making a comeback of his own. His voice could be heard on three of the ten songs on CHICAGO 18, and he is given co-writing credit for three, one of which he originally wrote

CHICAGO XVIII

over sixteen years earlier. Lamm explains that, before the band began the recording process for the new album, he urged everyone to get together informally. "I wrote a letter to everyone in the group," he states, "suggesting that we just get together and play. Not to rehearse or work up material, but just jam, like all bands are supposed to. We'd been working for so long under pressure, I thought that it might feel good to get back in touch with why we were together in the first place." Not a bad idea, considering they had a brand-new member playing two key roles, bass and vocals. Aside from Bill Champlin, Scheff was stepping into a band whose members had been together before he started grade school! While his approach to the music would certainly be fresh, there had to be a fair amount of fitting in to be worked on. Lamm makes the same point, "We played a lot of the old stuff, fooled around a lot and just kind of reconnected. At the same time Jason started getting a feel for being in the group, and when the time was right, we began stretching out with some new material."

CHICAGO 18 did not sound like 17, 16, or anything else, for that matter. The drums and the keyboards were very contemporary for 1986, but had lost the organic quality of the previous records. While Scheff played more bass than Cetera had chosen to on his last works, his sound was darker and less up-front. Peter Cetera had always brought a hybrid quality of Beatles and Motown to the music, whereas Scheff, from another era, was being truer to his roots, which, albeit different, fit the contemporary mix quite well.

Vocally, it was obvious from the first note of the first tune — Kipner and Caldwell's charming *Niagara Falls* — that Jason Scheff was trying to sound like Peter Cetera. Since *Niagara Falls* was the album's opener, Chicago and Foster may have leaned heavily on Scheff to mimic Cetera. "David said often to Jason, 'Sing as Cetera,'" Bill Champlin recalls. As the album unfolded, though, Scheff's mimicry was less blatant. Of Jason Scheff's first tour, Kiki Ebsen remembers that he was "very sweet, and a very talented musician and singer." She also recalls that the bassist needed to bring his vocals up to speed and give it his full attention. "He worked very hard on that tour," she says. "To be that young and have to go out there and basically be Peter Cetera was a ridiculously hard place for him to be. But he was so excited to be there. It was funny, he had to break out a Chicago songbook at the rehearsals!" Kiki also adds that the newcomer spiced things up a bit. "Jason had a lot of energy. He would run all over the stage, and he kicked a lot of new life into the band. He made everybody else kinda get up and put on a bigger show. And

FEELIN' STRONGER EVERY DAY

the women loved him. He was gorgeous! He was pretty dynamic on stage."

CHICAGO 18 entered the *Billboard* album charts at Number 82 on October 18, 1986, with the back cover of the magazine featuring a full-page ad for the record. The album peaked at Number 43. The first single released was an updated version of *25 Or 6 To 4*. With its half-time feel and computerized underscore, the song did not bode well with many of the band's original fans. Reworking a classic is a risky proposition, especially when the two most important elements of the original record — Cetera's voice and Kath's guitar — are gone. "David had an idea," recounts Robert Lamm. "He wanted to re-record one of our old hits. We went through our first five albums and eventually came up with *25 Or 6 To 4*. In a way, it's a touchstone for old Chicago fans, a way for them to connect to what we're doing now." Lamm underestimated the value of his earlier work in its original form. Perhaps a better idea would have been to take a song with less sense of heritage, like *In The Country* or *Free*, and re-design them for Jason and Bill. During November 1986, *25 Or 6 To 4* peaked at Number 37 on the charts. A music video, a la *Mission Impossible*, was produced for the song. Its rotation in the charts was short-lived.

The next single, however, was more in keeping with Chicago's current crop of hits. *Will You Still Love Me?* written by David Foster, Tom Keane and Richard Baskin, went all the way to Number 3. Sung by Jason Scheff and Bill Champlin, this ballad had all the winning qualities of the prior Foster/Chicago collaborations.

> Just say you love me for the rest of your life
> I gotta lot of love and I don't want to let go
> Will you still love me for the rest of my life?
> 'Cause I can't go on, no, I can't go on
> I can't go on if I'm on my own . . .
> — David Foster/Tom Keane/Richard Baskin, *Will You Still Love Me?* (ASCAP)

Jason Scheff began to breathe easier after *Will You Still Love Me?* became a hit. "When I first joined the band," says Scheff, "they put all of their confidence in me and never looked back. They invested in me as the future of the franchise. There were a lot of people who were skeptical. *Will You Still Love Me?* was a big hit, and then I finally felt comfortable that I was in."

The third single, *If She Would Have Been Faithful*, broke the Top 20 and

CHICAGO XVIII

landed at Number 14. Written by Steve Kipner and Randy Goodrum, the song was also sung by Scheff, and was in keeping with Chicago's strong adult contemporary style. The song had a similar appeal as CHICAGO 16's *Hard Habit To Break*, also penned by Kipner.

After the Donnie Dacus approach, the group may have realized that you cannot go too far away from home and still expect people, especially millions of them, to come along with you. Scheff worked hard to recreate the Cetera signature sound, and Bill Champlin, while he didn't try to copy Kath's vocal style, at least brought back a good portion of Chicago's classic sound.

The next step for the band was to hit the road with Jason Scheff and sell the new lead singer and bassist to the crowds. Kiki Ebsen joined the CHICAGO 18 tour midway through, subbing for the band's first MIDI-tech. "MIDI-tech, that was the title of the gig," she explains. Ebsen "jumped at the chance," to work with Chicago. "I wanted to get on the road," she continues. "I had never been on the road and I was trying to break in. Even though this wasn't an on-stage playing gig, it didn't matter. The money was great, and why not learn and see what it was all about? The downside was, I was very new to computers and had never played a sampler before, and that's what the gig was all about! I didn't know how to use the stuff, but I was a really good learner and a keyboard player. So I got the video and learned over night."

Chicago did not hire Kiki, and she didn't even have to audition. The young lady who held the position was actually "subletting" the gig to Ebsen, as she was pursuing other interests. "Apparently [Chicago] trusted her judgment in hiring me," she concludes. Kiki Ebsen learned all about the meaning of trial by fire. "My first gig was at the Bhudokan, in Japan," she remembers. "I kinda bluffed my way into the gig, and now I had to go to the first gig with no rehearsal, in an arena, and I'd never even been on an arena stage before. There's a lot of things to disorient you — the sound of the crowd and such — I was very nervous. Doing this type of gig was like being a lighting director; you had a lot of cues. One minute you're playing vocal samples on an Emulator, then, while you're reloading the next song, you may jump over to another keyboard to play a string part, and then turn back just in time to catch a part on the sequencer. Back then, you didn't have the luxury of these giant hard drives. MIDI was very new."

Ebsen got through the first gig almost unscathed. "We powered down before the show," she recounts, "and I forgot to turn the MIDI interface back on, so the sequence didn't start. When I figured out what was wrong, it was

FEELIN' STRONGER EVERY DAY

too late to turn the sequence on. It was a giant flub. After the show, I got called backstage and figured, 'This is it! First show, last show,' but the band just wanted to know what happened. I explained that I forgot to turn the interface on and they just said, 'That's it?' Apparently, the other girl who was doing this would launch into all this technical jargon and excuses, and the band was lost and would just say, 'Whatever!' So they were so impressed with my honesty that they ended up firing her and hiring me as their permanent MIDI-tech. There were no hard feelings, 'cause she was looking to leave the gig, anyway."

Publicity photo for release of NIGHT & DAY album:
Bill Champlin, Walter Parazaider, Jason Scheff, James Pankow, Tris Imboden, Lee Loughnane, Robert Lamm.

FEELIN' STRONGER EVERY DAY

Chicago keyboards with Bill Champlin, Lee Loughnane, and Robert Lamm during CHICAGO 19 Tour (top) and Jason Scheff (bottom).

CHICAGO XVIII

Keith Howland (top),
DaWayne Bailey (bottom).

FEELIN' STRONGER EVERY DAY

James Pankow, NIGHT & DAY Tour.

CHICAGO XIX

Robert Lamm (keyboards and lead vocals) ∾ Walter Parazaider (saxophone) ∾ Lee Loughnane (trumpet) ∾ James Pankow (trombone) ∾ Jason Scheff (lead vocals and bass) ∾ Danny Seraphine (drums, percussion, programming) Bill Champlin (keyboards, lead and background vocals)

∾

Additional Musicians: Chas Sanford (guitars) ∾ Charles Judge (keyboards) ∾ Peter Kaye (programming) ∾ Mike Murphy (drum tech, additional programming, cow bell) ∾ Kiki Ebsen (programming and keyboards) ∾ Peter Mayer (programming) ∾ Tamara Champlin (background vocals) ∾ Dan Huff (guitar) ∾ John Campbell (keyboards) ∾ Phillip Ashley (keyboards) ∾ Effran Toro (drum programming) ∾ DaWayne Bailey (guitars and background vocals)

Heart In Pieces
I Don't Wanna Live Without Your Love
I Stand Up
We Can Last Forever
Come In From The Night
Look Away
What Kind Of Man Would I Be?
Runaround
You're Not Alone
Victorious

For CHICAGO 19, Bill Champlin's formidable vocal talent finally came to the forefront. The singer sang all three of the album's hit singles, including the song that took the band to Number 1 for a third time. *Look Away*, a power-ballad written by Diane Warren, one of the most prominent songwriter's of the day, climbed the charts in record time and was the first hit single since *Saturday In The Park* to be sung by a Chicago member without a tenor voice. "Nobody knew that *Look Away* was Chicago," says Lee Loughnane. "We would play that song live, and you could see people saying, 'Why are they playing this? I didn't know they did this song. My God, it is them!' It wasn't registering because of what came before." Of his move to the frontline, Champlin simply says, "It was a blast. I got to use a different set of pipes."

Look Away, I Don't Wanna Live Without Your Love (also written by Diane Warren), and *You're Not Alone* were all hits — and all were ballads. Ballads truly were the strong suit on this record, and Chicago executed them beautifully. *What Kind Of Man Would I Be?*, written by Jason Scheff, Chas Sanford, and Bobby Caldwell, made perfect use of all of Chicago's attributes, including a moving instrumental horn solo section, and proved that Scheff was definitely in synch with his new band. Chicago was fast becoming ensconced in the burgeoning Adult Contemporary genre, much to the chagrin of some band members. Evidence that the group was still trying to break away from their association with the AC brand they felt had been put on them since *If You Leave Me Now* was their choice of Ron Nevison and Chas Sanford as CHICAGO 19's record producers. Nevison, who also played guitar on the album, had a long track record as engineer and producer for such major rock acts as Led Zeppelin, The Who, Bad Company, Heart, and Ozzy Osbourne. He also produced actor/singer Don Johnson's successful 1986 album, HEARTBEAT. Though the new album was propelled by its ballads, there were some respectable up-tempo tunes as well. *Heart In Pieces*, written by Tim Feehan and Brian MacLeod, and sung by Jason Scheff, featured some fine guitar work. And Robert Lamm's *I Stand Up*, written with Gerald McMann, was signature Chicago with a touch of R&B that harkened back to some of Lamm's earlier work.

Though the album spawned three Top-10 hits, CHICAGO 19 only reached Number 43 on the album chart, proof, perhaps, that Loughnane was right about diehard fans having difficulty associating the 'new sound' with the band. CHICAGO 19 was also the band's second album without a full-time guitarist. Besides Chas Sanford, guitarists, Dann Huff and DaWayne Bailey added their considerable talents to the record. Dann Huff, who has a list of session credits a mile long, has worked with artists as diverse as Engelbert Humperdink, Joe Cocker, Madonna, and Peter Cetera on his first post-Chicago solo release. Bailey, an L.A. session guitarist and singer, also contributed to Bob Seger's 1986 best seller, LIKE A ROCK. With all the changes taking place on record, Danny Seraphine decided to make some changes of his own. The drummer began experimenting more and more with the new MIDI technology and drum programming that had become commonplace in the music industry.

CHICAGO XIX

Kiki Ebsen was also recruited by Chicago to work on the CHICAGO 19 album and tour. "I was involved in a couple of days of programming and sequencing for CHICAGO 19," she remembers, "and I played some strings on *Look Away*. There were several people doing programming. I think the producers, Ron Nevison and Chas Sanford, had their own people." Ebsen, who was hidden behind the drum set for her first tour, says that Bill Champlin "campaigned for me to play a lot more. I actually played 70, 80 percent more on the CHICAGO 19 tour. I could be seen standing next to Bill. They didn't try to hide me, this time. Both Robert and Bill would step away from the keyboards and go out front to sing, and I would cover their part, be it piano or organ, and I did a lot of the string things that we used to sequence. I did them live, which had a better feel with the band, like all the stuff on *Hard Habit To Break*. It was a lot more fun the second time around." For the 19 tour, Kiki stayed on until the band went out for their second time around with The Beach Boys. "I was ready to move on by then," she recalls.

CHICAGO XX

GREATEST HITS 1982-1989

Peter Cetera ∾ Danny Seraphine ∾ Robert Lamm ∾ Bill Champlin ∾
Walter Parazaider ∾ James Pankow ∾ Lee Loughnane ∾ Jason Scheff

Hard To Say I'm Sorry/Get Away
Look Away
Stay the Night
Will You Still Love Me?
Love Me Tomorrow
What Kind Of Man Would I Be
You're The Inspiration
I Don't Wanna Live Without Your Love
Hard Habit To Break
Along Comes A Woman
If She Would Have Been Faithful
We Can Last Forever

Chicago's twentieth album became their third greatest hits package. The surprise here was the success of the Top-10 hit single, *What Kind Of Man Would I Be?* Originally released on CHICAGO 19, the song, written and sung by Jason Scheff, and co-written with Bobby Caldwell and Chas Sanford, reached Number 5 on the *Billboard* singles chart, giving Chicago a hit in the '90s. "With the success of *What Kind Of Man Would I Be?*, we now had hits in all four decades," exclaims Walter Parazaider.

> What kind of man would I be
> Living a life without any meaning
> And I know you could surely survive without me
> But if I had to live without you
> Tell me, what kind of man would I be...
> — Jason Scheff/Chas Sanford/Bobby Caldwell, *What Kind of Man Would I Be?* (ASCAP)

Released in November 1989, "Greatest Hits: 1982-1989" broke the Top 40 and settled at Number 37. Twenty years and twenty albums, four decades

CHICAGO XX

worth of hits, and Chicago was still a major force in the music industry in 1990. The band managed to survive two potentially catastrophic personnel changes, with Kath and Cetera, and was able to maneuver through and rise above Disco, Punk Rock, and New Wave, all of which claimed the lives of many stalwart bands. But while 1990 was the beginning of Chicago's fourth decade in the music business, it was also the end of the line for another original member of the band. Danny Seraphine, the man who had been there from day one, was fired from Chicago with hardly any explanation to the public.

"Danny was way into the MIDI thing," Kiki Ebsen recalls, and she feels he was responsible for creating the MIDI position she held with the band during the tours for CHICAGO 18 and 19, something the other members of the band questioned. "The MIDI-tech position was not easily embraced by the road crew," she recalls. "They didn't really understand it, since it never existed before. It made it very hard for me to step in." Bob Ludwig, who came back to work with Chicago for the 16, 17 and 18 album tours, remembers that period in time. "When we got to the Foster era, Danny was so intimidated by the whole thing that it got him on a downward spiral that he never recovered from. Electronic drums and sampling were real primitive. Foster wanted to start using the technology because it was something new. The other part of it was because Danny wasn't quite cutting it the way Foster wanted. So to compensate for that, Danny went out and got every kind of electronic equipment... samplers, you name it. He spent all day, every day dealing with programming. He got so wrapped up in the electronics that he just never practiced, never really played any more. On stage, he was playing more and more electronic drums. His solos were all samples and to some extent sounded awful. As things deteriorated more for Danny, it started rubbing the band the wrong way. The fact that he was losing his chops was affecting the band. Eventually that came to haunt him and they showed him the door."

Ebsen comments on Seraphine's last tour. "Danny was always very nice to me, very respectful, but he had a bad temper. When he felt that someone had screwed up or done something wrong," Kiki continues, "he flew off the handle, and I think his drum tech, Mike Murphy, took the brunt of it for a long time. When Danny got mad, you didn't want to be in his path." Seraphine admitted way back in 1974 during a *Down Beat* magazine interview that he was a hot head. "I'm notorious for punching walls but I don't like to hit people. It's just my Italian temper."

Ebsen also comments on the interpersonal dynamics between Seraphine and his bandmates. "I know there was a lot of tension between him and the other band members. Some of the things he was doing technically interfered with the show, like trying to start the sequences with his kick drum, and it just wasn't working, and he would blame the next person for it. It was painful because the band was really upset about it and they didn't understand why it was happening. They didn't know. They thought it was Mike or me, and we would say, 'You don't understand, if he even touches or makes noise with his bass drum pedal, it's gonna send a count and start the sequencer.' That happened so many times that Bill was furious — everybody was. It was not a good thing."

She remembers the end of her time on the 19 tour. "There were talks of Danny getting kicked out of the band. There was so much tension, it was inevitable, if Danny didn't agree himself, that he needed to A) to control his temper, and B) move on. Whatever came down took place after I left, but he was, in fact, gone after that tour."

For his part, Danny Seraphine claims he was a "casualty of corporate rock politics." Peter Cetera was under the impression that Seraphine was let go because he "didn't fit in with the current stage presentation." But Seraphine responded to that by saying that Cetera "probably didn't know what to say.... It was pretty embarrassing to do what they did to somebody who was with them for twenty-five years. I think that [Chicago] is somewhat ashamed of what they did and how it was done." He goes on to say that he would "need a chapter in a book to explain why [I'm not with Chicago anymore] without making it seem like I'm the complete victim." Unfortunately, he did not choose this book as his forum. "I wasn't a total innocent bystander," he admits, and concedes that his former band members are not bad guys, but "good guys who got misguided and made a mistake and got too far into it to change. Whether they'll admit that or not, I don't know."

Bill Champlin has been the most candid about the situation. By his account, Seraphine was not able to adjust musically to the direction that Chicago was going in, which fits with Bob Ludwig's take on the whole thing. "Danny will probably tell you that I got him fired," explains Champlin. "He was having a hard time locking in with the new rhythm section, especially on the ballads, and when I brought it up to the guys, they just ignored it, at first." Champlin claims that he eventually got the principal band members to take notice of the situation, and when Seraphine was confronted, he did not take the criticism lightly. "Those guys weighed the options, and that's when it hit the fan."

CHICAGO XX

Danny Seraphine was one of the most influential and respected pop drummers of the 1970s. He was among the legendary Buddy Rich's favorites, and, like Kath and Cetera, was always nominated, and often topped, many significant music polls. If he was, in fact, unable to groove with the new Chicago, it would probably have been because he did not want to take the time to work with the new musicians, especially Jason Scheff. While holding down the rhythm section with Peter Cetera for some seventeen years, it would have been especially difficult to jive with Scheff, a much younger bassist with a more modern approach to the instrument. Champlin did point out that sectional rehearsals were discussed with Seraphine, but they never materialized.

Danny Seraphine currently resides in Colorodo. In 1998, he produced an album called CHOCOLATE SOUP for the band Lyric. He also programmed all the drums and percussion.

Many fans were shocked to find out that Seraphine was no longer with Chicago, especially since the news of his departure was kept much quieter than Cetera's break. Some people only found out when they went to see the band live and realized that there was a different person behind the drum set. That person was former Kenny Loggins drummer, Tris Imboden. Born in Orange County, California, Imboden first heard Chicago play at the Shrine Auditorium in 1969. "I thought it was the greatest thing I'd ever heard," he recalls. "If somebody had told me then that one day I would be the drummer of that band, I would have said, 'Yeah, right! And I'm Napoleon!'" Twenty-one years later Bill Champlin asked him to join the band. "The timing was exquisite," remembers Imboden. "Gratefully, the chemistry amongst the band and myself was immediate. It was just really, really a great thing, musically and personality-wise, too."

Prior to joining Chicago, Tris's impressive list of credits included stints with Michael McDonald, Bob James, Richard Marx, Roger Daltrey, Chaka Kahn, Anita Baker, Stanley Clarke, Crosby, Stills & Nash, Julio Iglesias, and Neil Diamond. He also appeared on Peter Cetera's 1988 release, ONE MORE STORY, where he is credited for playing hi-hat on the tune, *Scheherazade* (which also featured Madonna using the alias Lulu Smith!) Of Tris' playing, Robert Lamm says, "I've never heard a louder drummer in my life." (Laughs) "The main thing he brings to our music is a real accurate time factor. Our repertoire is very large," Lamm continues, "and a lot of it shifts time signatures and such, so it's nice to know the pulse that you feel is being played." This is an interesting comment, in light of Champlin's assessment of Seraphine's alleged

FEELIN' STRONGER EVERY DAY

tribulations in his last days with the band.

Tris speaks of how he approached playing with Chicago, and his feelings about Danny Seraphine. "They've been playing some of their songs a long time," he states, "and rather than my always being the one to lean on, I have to be a little flexible and go with them. I also think Chicago's music is such a part of all of us, and Danny Seraphine having been a very influential drummer and such a stylist. What I really focused on was trying to maintain a certain degree of Danny's style, which I thought was an integral part of the music. At the same time, the band said they wanted me to make it my own, too. So I tried to pull things out that I thought were distinctly Danny, like the opening to *Saturday In The Park*, with those great fills that were sort of drum hooks that Danny came up with. But I allowed myself to come through as well."

Tris Imboden's first recording with the band was CHICAGO 21, his "unofficial" debut. Although he had been asked to join the band, he was not credited as a band member, but as an "additional musician" along with fellow drummer John Keane.

During the CHICAGO 19 tour, another guitarist, DaWayne Bailey, had been added to the band, as Kiki Ebsen recalls. "He was completely on another planet with his playing. I loved it." Ebsen herself left the tour on good terms. She was proud to be a part of the band's history. "I would be out on a day off," she says, "and the radio would play a Chicago retrospective, and I'd think, 'My God! I work for them!' I was amazed!" In retrospect, she comments that "Chicago really didn't need all the bells and whistles, except for maybe on the glossier tunes." She felt that the band, and Seraphine in particular, wanted to stay on the cutting edge and make sure that their sound was current. She was very impressed with their keyboard sounds, which she says gave the songs a "Shimmer, that big David Foster-y sound." After leaving Chicago, Kiki Ebsen carved out quite an impressive career as a keyboard player and background vocalist for such major artists as Al Jarreau, James Ingram, Jeffrey Osborne, Belinda Carlisle, Boz Scaggs, and Christopher Cross. A formidable singer/songwriter and musician, she has recorded two solo albums, RED in 1993 and AVENUES in 1997.

But Ebsen's affiliation with Chicago would eventually come around again. In 1994, she joined Bill Champlin for a month-long tour of Scandanavia in support of his solo album, and he started to sing. "That was a great tour, and a great band," Kiki recalls. "I fell in love with Bill all over again. He's one of my idols. He's an amazing player and a great guy." Music from that

CHICAGO XX

Scandanavian tour was released as a live album available on Champlin's website (http://members.aol.com/tamaracham/index.html). Then in 1995 Ebsen joined Peter Cetera for his first-ever solo tour. "He was great," she is quick to say. "It was an amazing band." She did not get the gig because of her ties to Chicago or Bill Champlin but through her friend Scott Plunkett. "He was the MD, and the main keyboard player, and he lined up the audition." It was certainly a plus that Ebsen was a female with a great voice, since much of Cetera's solo material was comprised of female vocal duets and harmonies. "Peter had a lot of ladies on that tour," Ebsen says, laughing. "There was a female sax player and singer that he was producing out of Nashville, and Mindy Stein was also singing backup and taking the duets." Stein toured with Fleetwood Mac and Stevie Nicks, among others. Ebsen says that Peter Cetera was a pleasure to work with. "Peter has a certain star quality that can be intimidating, but he's a real teddy bear. He loved the band and he loved being on the road. He really cared about us. Although a lot of the gigs got canceled, the ones we did were superb. Peter was nervous, since he hadn't toured in so long, but he never sounded better. His voice was just great."

The canceled gigs were due, in part, to the fact that Cetera did not wish to promote himself or the gigs with any connections to his former band. "Peter didn't want to talk about Chicago," Kiki explains. "He didn't want to fall back on it or use it as a vehicle to get his thing happening."

The band did wind up playing several Chicago songs on the road, though. "We played *Feelin' Stronger Every Day*," recalls Kiki, *Happy Man, If You Leave Me Now, and 25 Or 6 To 4*." Ebsen remembers that Cetera chose those tunes because he wanted to "play bass and just have fun."

In June 1999, Kiki Ebsen got a phone call from Bill Champlin who asked her to sub for him on a Chicago gig. "I was floored," she admits. "I was so honored that he would offer that to me, but it happened to be for June 12, which was the day I was getting married!" She politely declined... the gig, not the wedding. "I'm still able to say that I'm really the only female associated with their music."

These were turbulent times for old Chicago band members and road crew like Bob Ludwig, who, like Danny Seraphine, was released by the band. Ludwig speculates on why he was let go. "When Bill came into the band, he would come up to me and say, 'Whatever you're doing to Peter's voice, you should do to my voice. My voice sucks (in the mix), and his sounds great!' Some of what I did for Peter worked for Bill, but some didn't. Bill had a raspy voice and Peter's was more melodic and polished. I tried to explain to Bill that certain effects didn't work for him and that we would have to do something else. That kind of started a little friction between he and I. I felt that he never quite gave me the opportunity to do what I felt was best for the band, from a sound point of view as a whole, not concentrating on his sound only. He used to think that I would only concentrate on Peter, but the songs were arranged around Peter, written around Peter, and Peter wrote a lot of them. And that's why it had that Peter center! Bill wrote a couple of songs and they were great. We just happened to do more of Peter's than Bill's, which never became hits."

In the end, Bob feels that the new regime thought it best that the two parties came to a parting of the ways. "I used to mix the band the way they used to sound on record. I went to great lengths to maintain that sound. When Peter left, and they got rid of Chris Pinnick, they told me that they wanted someone who had never heard them before to mix them because they wanted to go in a different direction musically and they wanted a different kind of sound. They said I knew the music too well and couldn't deviate from that, and to some extent, that may be true. But I can't help but think that was an excuse to say, 'Hey, Bob, we don't like the way you're mixing anymore.' So now they wanted somebody else. We all went into a room — it was Lamm and Champlin and Pankow — the whole band except Danny was in the room. Lamm and Pankow said 'We're gonna have a whole new sound with more keyboards.' This is also when they got DaWayne Bailey to play guitar. It was okay but it was more David Foster than Chicago. Even the original stuff never sounded the same after that, because they weren't playing it the same, and someone else was mixing. I remained on a working level with the band for several years after that, providing them with sound equipment, which I eventually sold to Maryland Sound." Bob hold no grudges and still sees some of the band members on a regular basis. Like many others — long-time Chicago fans and band members — he recognized that the sound of Chicago had changed.

CHICAGO XXI

REPRISE 26391

Jason Scheff (bass, lead vocals, background vocals) ∾ Walter Parazaider (saxophone, flute, background vocals) ∾ James Pankow (trombone, background vocals) ∾ Lee Loughnane (trumpet, flugelhorn, background vocals) ∾ Bill Champlin (keyboards, lead vocals, background vocals) ∾ Robert Lamm (keyboards, lead vocals, background vocals) ∾ DaWayne Bailey (guitar, background vocals)

∾

John Keane (drums) ∾ Robbie Buchanan (keyboards) ∾ Effrain Toro (keyboards) ∾ Tom Keane (keyboards) ∾ Steve Porcaro (keyboard programming) ∾ Michael Landau (guitar) ∾ Steven "Doc" Kupka (horns) ∾ David Foster (piano) ∾ Tris Imboden (drums)

Explain It To My Heart
If It Were You
You Come To My Senses
Somebody Somewhere
What Does It Take
One From The Heart
Chasin' The Wind
God Save The Queen
Man To Woman
Only Time Can Heal The Wounded
Who Do You Love
Holdin' On

CHICAGO 21 was the band's first studio follow-up to the highly successful 19 album. The band tried to repeat history by hiring Ron Nevison to produce and engineer the album, and they even brought in Humberto Gatica, the other half of David Foster's team responsible for CHICAGO 16 and 17, to produce, engineer, and mix the first single. Chicago again turned to songwriter Diane Warren, who contributed two songs, *Explain It To My Heart*, the ballad the band was counting on to carry the record, and *Chasin' The Wind*, the Bill Champlin vocal vehicle that was also used in the Tom Cruise movie, *Days of Thunder*. Also back on board, and this time added to the lineup as their new guitarist, was DaWayne Bailey, who had been Chicago's recording and touring sideman. Bailey brought a distinctly '90s sound to Chicago. His playing was a mix of Joe Satriani, Steve Vai, and Steve Lukather. His use of effects, especially the guitar synthesizer, gave the live shows an added dimension that was aurally exciting. While he tended to be a bit "far out," as Bill Champlin put it, he did keep some elements of Terry Kath's sound and style alive.

CHICAGO 21 was Jason Scheff's third studio album with the group and Bill Champlin's fifth. The new band was beginning to find their identity more on this record. There was a definite energy and spark on XXI that was only hinted at on the previous two albums. Scheff's vocals took on a new depth and dynamic range. He no longer sounded like a guy trying to pass himself off as the new Peter Cetera. And since this was the first album without Danny Seraphine, there must have been an inherent energy and excitement in working with 'new energy' behind the drums.

But for all the things right with CHICAGO 21, there was also a lot wrong. The up-tempo songs worked like a charm. *If It Were You*, written by Jason Scheff, Darrin Scheff, and Tony Smith, and *Who Do You Love*, written by Bill Champlin and Dennis Matkosky, are both good examples of the new band's ability to rise above the old image and create a signature sound of their own, while still keeping it very familiar by letting the horn section do what they do best. But those songs were the exception. CHICAGO XXI was loaded with ballads, and not one of them was a hit. By rights, the two Diane Warren songs, *Explain It To My Heart* and *Chasin' The Wind*, should have been hit singles, but that didn't happen. "Those first two singles were really nice songs," says Jason Scheff, "but you're releasing something that you're going to try and top songs like *Hard Habit To Break* and *What Kind Of Man Would I Be?* Ironically, Chicago's long-term success made radio resistant to the new music. We were competing with ourselves." In Lee Loughnane's opinion, *Explain It To My Heart* "was the best Diane Warren song that I'd ever heard up to that time. It was gorgeous and it was in our style. I still think to this day that it was a number one record."

CHICAGO XXI, released in January 1991, peaked at Number 66 in March, but by May 4th, the album was gone from the charts, which were being ruled

CHICAGO XXI

by Vanilla Ice, M.C. Hammer, Madonna, and newcomer, Mariah Carey. Robert Lamm looks back on the aftermath of CHICAGO 21 and says, "We considered the possibility that perhaps it was better to succeed or fail on our own merits." Even though CHICAGO XXI broke the band's post-Cetera winning streak, 1991 was the year that Chicago was given a star on the renowned Hollywood Walk of Fame. With a new guitarist, a new drummer, and a new-found respect for their own judgment, Chicago was ready to move on to the next project, the notorious STONE OF SISYPHUS album.

CHICAGO XXII

THE STONE OF SISYPHUS

Bill Champlin ∾ Jason Scheff ∾ James Pankow ∾ Walter Parazaider ∾
Robert Lamm ∾ Tris Imboden ∾ DaWayne Bailey

All The Years
The Stone Of Sisyphus
Bigger Than Elvis
Sleeping In The Middle Of The Bed Again
Mah Jong
Let's Take A Lifetime
The Pull
Candle For The Dark
Plaid
Cry For The Lost
Get On This
The Show Must Go On

In Chicago's long history of making records, there were probably one or two albums that the band wished would vanish from existence. (Carnegie Hall, anyone?) So imagine the band's surprise when they finally got to make a record that provided them with an honest representation of their creative energies, only to have their record label refuse to release it because the label executives felt it didn't sound like Chicago 'should sound'. That is the story of THE STONE OF SISYPHUS, Chicago's twenty-second studio album, and their second record to sport a name, not a number.

The album was produced by Peter Wolf. Wolf had studied classical piano at the conservatory in Vienna, Austria, and won an award at the European Jazz Festival at age 16. He played keyboard for Frank Zappa and The Mothers of Invention from 1976-1980, then produced the Jefferson Starship smash hit album KNEE DEEP IN HOOPLA in 1985. In 1986 he produced four Number 1 records: *We Built this City* and *Sara* by Jefferson Starship, *Everybody Have Fun Tonight* by Wang Chung, and *Who's Johnny* by El Debarge. He also produced

CHICAGO XXII

and arranged hits for The Commodores, Heart, Foreigner, Kenny Loggins, Go West, and The Pointer Sisters.

For THE STONE OF SISYPHUS sessions, producer Peter Wolf's plan was to have the band approach the record like they did in the early days. He suggested that the band members prepare all the material themselves and experiment with everything. "Peter told me, 'I want you to bring over your bass clarinet, all your saxes, your flutes, everything,'" remembers Walt Parazaider. "He said, 'We're gonna use everything the way you used to in the old days.' That was very exciting to all of us." Parazaider felt that Chicago needed to break out of their 'ballad prison' and that THE STONE OF SISYPHUS was the answer. "That was a record that had to be made," he declares. The saxophonist also felt that the band might not have stayed together had Sisyphus not been made. "We were frustrated," he says, "that we weren't doing what we wanted to do, cranking out things that Warner Bros. wanted us to do that sold. We're not looking a gift horse in the mouth, a hit is a hit is a hit, but there was other stuff for us to say, and that's where SISYPHUS comes in."

Musically, STONE OF SISYPHUS was the most daring and satisfying Chicago album in many years, perhaps since CHICAGO III. The musicianship was superb, and the new band was running on all cylinders. With this album, Chicago's current lineup, which now officially included drummer Tris Imboden, had finally broken away from the ghosts of Chicago past. Perhaps that's why Warner Bros. was reticent to accept the album for release. "Warner Bros. didn't get the record," states Parazaider. "They didn't like it so much, they thought that maybe we should part ways, which we did."

The album was definitely a departure for Chicago. Of the twelve tunes, there were only three ballads, and two of those owed more to Earth, Wind & Fire than Bread. The one true 'Chicago style' ballad, Jason Scheff's *Bigger Than Elvis*, contained the records only schmaltz, but considering that it's a touching tribute to his father, Jerry Scheff, who played bass for Elvis and was on the road more than he was at home with his son, it can be forgiven. Ballads aside, SISYPHUS contained elements of Rap (yes, Rap on a Chicago record!), Urban dance beats, Hip-Hop, and a whole lot of Rock, R&B, and Funk. There is a lot of Robert Lamm on the record. The man who had gone creatively AWOL for quite some time obviously appreciated Peter Wolf's invitation to make a record without the restrictions of such heavy-handed producers as Guercio and Foster. There is also a lot of Bill Champlin on SISYPHUS. His enormous talents are omnipresent, and his influence breathes life into all the R&B and funk-flavored songs. And guitarist DaWayne Bailey, who co-wrote the title track with Lee Loughnane, as well as *Get On This* with James Pankow, sings and plays more than ever before, giving Chicago a new texture. *Get On This* is not your typical Chicago fare.

> In the middle of a dream
> Thought I saw the sacred Love Supreme
> So beautiful yet so obscene
> But I'm not sure I'm sleeping
>
> And in a golden sun
> I saw Hitler, Elvis, and angels
> A little baby with a big gun
> I saw Jesus kissing the devil
>
> — James Pankow, Felicia Parazaider, DaWayne Bailey, *Get On This* (ASCAP)

While the album dismayed the folks at Warner Bros., Peter Wolf accomplished his goal. SISYPHUS came off like the Chicago albums of yore, where each writer and singer and musician's individuality and personality came shining through on every song. And while fans of the original band may have raised their collective eyebrows, too bad. This version of Chicago deserved to speak its mind and be heard. After all, what was Chicago, if not a band that always dared to be different and break new ground. If STONE OF SISYPHUS had been released, Chicago just may have gone the way of The Grateful Dead and existed outside the mainstream, leading their legions of fans in all-night music fests, playing new music that needn't be written and recorded for the sole purpose of chart fuel.

Some of the tunes on SISYPHUS have surfaced on Chicago's import albums, like the Canadian release, OVERTIME, and a European GREATEST HITS package. Jason Scheff re-recorded the song *Mah Jhong* for his 1998 solo album, CHAUNCEY. Parazaider is still optimistic that SISYPHUS may see the light of day. "The master tapes weren't burnt," he says, "This thing will get released." But it certainly didn't get released in 1993, and now that Warner Bros. was out of the picture, Chicago was once again in need of a game plan.

CHICAGO XXIII

NIGHT & DAY (BIG BAND)

GIANT 24615

Robert Lamm (keyboards and vocals) ～ Lee Loughnane (trumpet and flugelhorn) ～ James Pankow (trombone) ～ Walter Parazaider (woodwinds) ～ Bill Champlin (keyboards, guitar, vocals) ～ Jason Scheff (bass, vocals) ～ Tris Imboden (drums and harmonica) ～ Bruce Gaitsch (guitar)

～

Guests: The Gipsy Kings, ～ Jade, Joe Perry, ～ Paul Shaffer ～ Luis Corte, ～ Jack Duncan, ～ Sal Ferreras (percussion)

Chicago
Caravan
Dream A Little Dream Of Me
Goody Goody
Moonlight Serenade
Night & Day
Blues In The Night
Sing, Sing, Sing
Sophisticated Lady
In The Mood
Don't Get Around Much Anymore
Take The "A" Train

With the STONE OF SISYPHUS album in limbo, and their immediate relationship with Warner Bros. over, Chicago moved on to the next phase of their career by taking up with one of Warner's affiliates, Giant Records. The band's one and only album for Giant was 1995s NIGHT & DAY (BIG BAND), Chicago's glorious tribute to big band and swing music.

While the record was a departure for Chicago, it was even more so for producer Bruce Fairbairn, who until now, had been known for his work with major rock acts AC/DC, Aerosmith, Van Halen, and Bon Jovi. In fact, Aerosmith's lead guitarist, Joe Perry, contributed guitar to one of tracks, the Johnny Mercer/Harold Arlen classic *Blues In The Night*. "We sent Joe a tape and he recorded his part," says Lee Loughnane. "He really brought that song alive."

Fairbairn was credited with "out of tune 2nd trumpet" on the album's first cut, composer Fred Fisher's *Chicago*. "He's actually a trumpet player who played in Vancouver growing up," explains Loughnane of Bruce Fairbairn. "He played Chicago and Blood, Sweat & Tears songs when he was a kid, so he was familiar with our music. On the surface, it seems like a strange pairing, but he really supported us. He's very musical. He's good with vocals and brass, and obviously, he's good with guitars and drums." Bill Champlin recalls working with Fairbairn. "Bruce is a cool guy," says Champlin. "He's a lot more sensitive a musician than the records he's done would seem to indicate. He's done some real slammin' rock and roll records, all of which are really good." Sadly, Bruce Fairbairn died in March 1999 at his home in Vancouver, British Columbia.

NIGHT & DAY gave everyone in the band a chance to stretch out, especially the horn section. "Pankow, Lee Loughnane, and Walt Parazaider definitely had their work cut out for them with this record," admits Bill Champlin. "Horns were the vocals of the time," says big band enthusiast Lee Loughnane of the Swing Era." Then rock and roll came out and the guitar became the lead voice for a long time. And then Chicago comes, and we try to make the horns the lead voice again, and we've been pretty successful at it."

Although NIGHT & DAY didn't burn up the charts – it entered at Number 106 on June 10, 1995, and peaked at Number 90 just one week later – the album was a personal triumph for the band. "We had so much fun doing this," says James Pankow. "It was total freedom, especially for us horn guys," though he's well aware of the album's limitations. "This isn't the kind of album that's gonna sell like Hootie and the Blowfish," he remarks, referring to the band that held the number one album spot at the time NIGHT & DAY was released. He claims that the album's word of mouth has been positive and that sales have shot up in towns where the band has been playing live. "Maybe we'll never get back in the Top 10 again, or be the 'flavor of the month' again," Pankow reasons, "but we're happy to be making music we believe in once again and kicking butt on stage. We're also seeing more smiles in the audience than I remember seeing in years. You don't know how gratifying that is."

For NIGHT & DAY, Chicago was joined by several guest stars, including the

CHICAGO XXIII

Gipsy Kings, who added their soulful Flamenco sound to the band's arrangement of Louis Prima's *Sing, Sing, Sing*. Also on hand were the female vocal group, Jade, who sang in duet with Jason Scheff on the lovely *Dream A Little Dream Of Me*, written by Gus Kahn, Wilbur Schwandt, and Fabian Andre. Also making a guest appearance was David Letterman's eccentric piano genius, Paul Shaffer, who added his "piano stylings" to the previously mentioned tune and wrote the album's liner notes.

NIGHT & DAY was certainly not as radically different as STONE OF SISYPHUS, but it was not a typical Chicago album by any means. It was obvious that the band was turning its collective attention away, for the time being, from their preoccupation with making hits. Everyone sounded great on this record. Robert Lamm gave true Chicago fans cause to celebrate by singing eight of the twelve tunes on the record – six as lead vocalist, or co-lead vocalist, and two with the ensemble, his biggest showing in many years. Bill Champlin sang three songs, giving a dose of R&B that fans of the new Chicago had come to expect. His take on the Johnny Mercer/Matty Malneck classic, *Goody Goody*, and the Duke Ellington/Bob Russell standard, *Don't Get Around Much Anymore*, were cool enough to turn just about anybody into fans of the genre. With such homage paid to Benny Goodman, Duke Ellington, Count Basie, Glenn Miller, and Cole Porter, one can't help but wonder if this album might have put a smile on James William Guercio's face, as he had always felt that Chicago should have pursued this avenue.Chicago had appeared on a television special in the early '70s hosted by Duke Ellington. The band greeted Ellington, telling him what an honor it was to be on the show. "I'll never forget what he said to us," says James Pankow. "He said, 'Boys, it's my honor and pleasure, because you are the next Duke Ellingtons.' We never forgot that, especially since he died only three weeks after that."

Aiding the Chicago horn section on NIGHT & DAY was legendary jazz musician Bill Watrous and his orchestra. Watrous, a revered trombonist and bandleader of the jazz-rock group Ten Wheel Drive, made some highly acclaimed albums of his own throughout the 1970s.

One more change that took place during the creation of the new album was the dismissal of DaWayne Bailey as Chicago's guitarist. Bailey's caffeinated, whammy-bar style would have been notably out of place here. Due to some unpublicized problems between Bailey and Walt Parazaider, Chicago decided to part-company with Mr. Bailey. The guitar chair, at least for this album, was effectively filled by studio honcho Bruce Gaitsch, whose long list of credits

FEELIN' STRONGER EVERY DAY

included sessions with Madonna, Poco, Richard Marx, The Fixx, Celine Dion, Bill Champlin, Peter Cetera, and The Muppets. After NIGHT & DAY, Chicago's revolving door policy for guitarists was again in effect.

In 1995, the band scheduled two days of auditions to find their fifth guitarist. As usual, the band eschewed going with a big name and opted for talent and temperament. Born in Silver Springs, Maryland, on August 14, 1964, Keith Howland became the newest member of the "Chicago guitar club," a phrase coined by DaWayne Bailey. But Howland was not on the group's list of potentials. He earned the coveted spot by stalking the band. "They had a firm list of guys they were going to listen to," says Howland. "I actually heard that they were looking for a guitar player through a friend of mine who happened to be working in the building where the auditions were being held." Keith contacted HK Management and was told that the auditions were closed. "As a last ditch effort, I just drove down there and sat in the parking lot, waiting for the band to show up," he recalls. The first guy to pull up was Jason Scheff, whom Howland had met once before when the bassist came to see a band that Keith was playing in. Howland reintroduced himself to Scheff and asked if there was any chance he could get an audition. "He told me to go on home because they were full that day," he recalls, "but that he would talk to the guys." Scheff called Howland later that same day and told him that Chicago had added a third day of auditions just to hear him. "I went down, and I was the only guy to play that day," says Howland. "I was so nervous, it was ridiculous. I played through some tunes with them, did some *a cappella* background vocals with Bill, Jason and Robert. We finished, and I started packing up my gear. They all went into the hallway and were talking. Bill came walking back in and said, 'Hey, you want a gig?'"

For Keith Howland, Chicago wasn't just a gig, it was *the* gig. "My older brother was the first one that turned me on to the band, actually," he says. Howland, who began playing guitar at seven, named Terry Kath as one of his earliest influences. Howland came to Los Angeles after graduating college in 1988 and worked with Patty Smyth and Rick Springfield. The Chicago gig is the biggest break he has ever had, and he says that he will stay "for the duration, as long as they'll have me."

It was his love of the band and Terry Kath's playing that gave Keith the edge and landed him the membership. "When Keith made the audition," says Walt Parazaider, "he played so much of the inside stuff and the rhythm stuff like Terry did that he was the guy. You just knew he was the guy to do this."

CHICAGO XXIII

Howland's playing has not only been embraced by the band but the fans as well, who feel that the guitarist's respect for Kath is keeping the classic Chicago sound alive. "It didn't seem right for me to play it any other way because that was the way I had always heard it," says Howland. Not only has he managed to incorporate many of Kath's recorded solos and guitar parts into his own playing, but Keith has also been able to recreate a lot of the late guitarist's sounds. With Howland in place, Chicago's live sound is the best it's been in many years.

For the NIGHT & DAY tour, Chicago employed drum tech/MIDI pro Chris Ralles to run the samplers. Ralles, who has toured as a tech with some of music's biggest names, including Madonna, Michael McDonald, and Kenny Loggins, got the gig through his association with Tris Imboden. "Tris and I became friends when he was playing with Kenny Loggins," states Ralles, who started working for Loggins in 1987 and is now entering his fourteenth year with the singer. Imboden re-joined the band in 1988. "He's a great drummer and a great guy," he continues. "I saw him at a NAMM show and he asked me if I would tech for him with Chicago." Ralles is also a top-notch drummer and percussionist, and has used those talents with Dave Mason, Michael McDonald, the Rembrandts, Dave Koz, and, on occasion, Kenny Loggins. "I'm a big fan of Tris Imboden's drumming. He was the reason I said yes and got involved with the Chicago tour. He's a good friend, " declares Chris. "And he was made for that band. There are other guys who could have done it, but Tris was definitely the right choice. And he loves the gig."

Ralles' duties as drum tech also included running sequences for the band, something they relied on heavily for the NIGHT & DAY songs they performed live. "They had extra horns, background vocals, and keyboard parts running during the big band stuff," says Chris. As the band learned during the '80s, MIDI and samples are not without their downside. Chris Ralles remembers a particularly embarrassing moment toward the end of his run on the tour. "I ended up with the wrong set list on the drum riser, and I, personally, had the wrong set list," he recalls. "We were doing two shows a night at Caesar's in Las Vegas, and they told me it was a short set, so I grabbed the short set list and showed it to the horn tech, who said, 'Yeah, that's the short set list.' The set started and the first song was right. The second tune in, Tris counted it off and half the band knew that it was wrong but went with it . . . they were right in, Jason, Keith, Bill . . . basically everybody except the horn players knew what was going on. They were kinda lost. When Tris motioned to me that it was

FEELIN' STRONGER EVERY DAY

the wrong set list, I ran back to the computer to try and get it in line with the real order, but by the time I was able to grab the right set list and get back to the computer. I wasn't ready for it, and Tris yelled 'Go,' so I hit go and it was the wrong song!" Ralles laughs now, but says the experience was "No fun" when it happened. To add to his nightmare, each of the horn players, one by one, came up to him backstage and "as politely as possible, pretty much reamed me! After the show I went backstage and apologized to everyone. That's the problem with that type of technology." He is also glad that the incident didn't affect his friendship with Imboden. "Whenever I see Tris, we're still buds," says Ralles.

Chris says that the rest of his six-months with the band, which included trips to Canada and Japan, was great. "We did a great gig at the Ford Theater in Washington," he says. "It was the President's Gala, for Bill Clinton. Chicago played, and so did Shania Twain. That was actually right before the NIGHT & DAY tour." Ralles' stint with Chicago coincided with Keith Howland's first tour. "Keith did a great job," says Chris. "He played everything perfectly, his vocals were right on, they made a great choice with him." As Ralles remembers, "the music sounded great every night," though he adds a qualification about the volume on stage. "You wouldn't think it, but the volume on stage was really loud, especially where I was, on Bill Champlin's side of the stage where his Leslie was. I think he had it beefed up to be extra loud," he laughs. "I think it went to fifteen or twenty!"

In 1996, Chicago took the big step toward total autonomy and started their own record label, Chicago Records, Inc. The band acquired the rights to their masters and re-released their previous works on the new label. In addition, Chicago put out a Terry Kath tribute album called CHICAGO PRESENTS THE INNOVATIVE GUITAR OF TERRY KATH. The record contained fourteen songs that prominently featured Kath's talents as a singer, songwriter, and guitarist. While none of Bill Champlin's solo albums are available on the label, Chicago Records does offer releases from both Robert Lamm and Jason Scheff, including Lamm's original CBS debut, SKINNY BOY.

CHICAGO XXIV

Robert Lamm ∽ Lee Loughnane ∽ James Pankow ∽ Walter Parazaider
∽ Terry Kath ∽ Peter Cetera ∽ Danny Seraphine ∽ Bill Champlin ∽
Jason Scheff ∽ Tris Imboden ∽ Keith Howland

THE HEART OF CHICAGO, 1967-1997, VOLUME I

REPRISE 46554-2

You're The Inspiration
If You Leave Me Now
Make Me Smile
Hard Habit To Break
Saturday In The Park
Wishin' You Were Here
The Only One
Colour My World

Look Away
Here In My Heart
Just You 'N Me
Does Anybody Really Know
  What Time It Is?
Will You Still Love Me?
Beginnings
Hard To Say I'm Sorry/Get Away

THE HEART OF CHICAGO, 1967-1998, VOLUME II

REPRISE 46911-2

Dialogue (Part 1 & 2)
Old Days
All Roads Lead To You
Love Me Tomorrow
Baby, What A Big Surprise
You're Not Alone
What Kind Of Man
  Would I Be
No Tell Lover

Show Me A Sign
(I've Been) Searchin' So Long
Call On Me
I Don't Wanna Live Without
  Your Love
Feelin' Stronger Every Day
Stay The Night
I'm A man
25 Or 6 To 4

In 1997, Reprise records released the HEART OF CHICAGO, 1967-1997, a greatest hits package which also contained two new songs. *Here In My Heart*, sung by Bill Champlin and written by James Newton Howard and

FEELIN' STRONGER EVERY DAY

Glen Ballard, was released as a single and placed high on *Billboard*'s Adult Contemporary chart, proving that Chicago was still a viable, albeit reluctant, AC act. *The Only One*, written by James Pankow and Greg O'Conner, was produced by Lenny Kravitz, who also added vocals to the ensemble mix. With the help of Kravitz' knack for all things retro, this song captured a lot of the band's old glory, including a great wah-wah guitar track, the trademark of the late Terry Kath.

Volume II also contained two bonus tracks, a very popular move by many artists issuing greatest hits packages. It was a good way to increase interest in the old stuff while somewhat guaranteeing a sale for the new stuff. The overtly commercial *Show Me A Sign*, by Pankow and O'Conner, received modest radio play, and featured Jason Scheff singing in the stratosphere. *All Roads Lead To You*, written by Marc Beeson and Desmond Child, saw some chart action, and gave Champlin another vocal credit. Bruce Springsteen's E-Street Band keyboard player, Roy Bittan, produced both songs.

CHICAGO XXV

THE CHRISTMAS ALBUM

CRD 3035

Jason Scheff (vocals, electric bass, electric upright bass, fretless bass, computer programming) ⚡ Bill Champlin (vocals, keyboards, synth organ, synth vibes, electric piano, synth bass, guitar) ⚡ Lee Loughnane (vocals, trumpet, flugelhorn, piccolo trumpet, muted trumpet) ⚡ James Pankow (trombone) ⚡ Walter Parazaider (tenor and alto sax, C flute, alto flute) ⚡ Robert Lamm (vocals, electric piano, piano) ⚡ Tris Imboden (drums)

⚡

Additional Musicians: Tim Pierce (guitars) ⚡ Luis Conte (percussion) ⚡ Roy Bittan (accordian, keyboards) ⚡ George Black (computer programming)

Background Vocals: Alex Brown, Tamara Champlin, Alvin Chea, Gia Ciambotti, H.K. Dorsey, Gary Falcone, Edie Lehmann-Boddicker, Bobbie Page, Carmen Twilie, Oren Waters, Maxine Waters-Willard, Mona Lisa Young

Children's Choir: Amity Addrisi, Michael Amezcua, Alex Bittan, Ryan Bittan, Clark Gable, Kayley Gable, Kate Lamm, Sean Lamm, Dylan Loughnane, River Loughnane, Sarah Pankow, Brittanay Scott, Jade Thacker

Little Drummer Boy	Santa Claus Is Coming To Town
God Rest Ye Merry Gentlemen	Christmas Time Is Here
Have Yourself A Merry Little Christmas	Let It Snow! Let It Snow! Let It Snow!
The Christmas Song	What Child Is This
O Come All Ye Faithful	White Christmas
Child's Prayer	Silent Night
Feliz Navidad	One Little Candle

CHICAGO 25 — or XXV — or "The Christmas Album," as it's become known — was the first studio release for the band on its own label, Chicago Records, Inc. Released in 1998, the album is the Christmas equivalent of NIGHT & DAY. The band has given the Chicago treatment to such

FEELIN' STRONGER EVERY DAY

holiday classics as *The Little Drummer Boy, God Rest Ye Merry Gentlemen, Silent Night,* and *Let It Snow.* "Thirty years ago," says Walter Parazaider, "we decided that a Christmas album would be something that's a legacy, something that could return every year. But we worked so much in those first five years – 300 days a year – that we never got around to it."

CHICAGO XXV was produced by Roy Bittan, whom the band obviously enjoyed working with on their two HEART OF CHICAGO records. Bittan kept Chicago focused on the task of recording the album by decorating the recording studio in a holiday motif. "There were Christmas lights strung around the room and poinsettias everywhere," says Lee Loughnane.

As was the case on NIGHT & DAY, everything from R&B and rock, to funk and swing is employed here. Bill Champlin's reworking of *Santa Claus Is Coming To Town* sounds like Steely Dan meets Ray Charles. Jason Scheff's rendition of *God Rest Ye Merry Gentlemen* implies Sting, while Robert Lamm's arrangement of the Jose Feliciano classic, *Feliz Navidad,* shows that Chicago does, in fact, recognize their own signature sound. The latter is filled with instrumental passages reminiscent of Chicago's movements from the band's earliest albums. The song shows just how valuable Lamm is to the integrity of the band. The record's single, the Kahn/Styne favorite *Let It Snow! Let It Snow! Let It Snow!,* features a lead vocal by Lee Loughnane, who hasn't been up front on the mic since CHICAGO XI. Loughnane could be heard singing the song in concert, as well as on a number of television appearances, including the *Tonight Show* and the 1998 Macy's Thanksgiving Day Parade. Loughnane also contributed the album's only original song, *Child's Prayer.* Written along with John Durrill, the song is sung by a choir that includes the children of Loughnane, Pankow, Lamm, and producer Roy Bittan.

"We looked at a lot of other Christmas albums over the last few years," says Robert Lamm, "and realized it's pretty difficult to write something of the caliber of *The Christmas Song* or *White Christmas.* There's a reason those songs are standards. The one written by Lee is extraordinary and has a lot of credibility. Believe me, it wouldn't have been included if it couldn't stand up to the rest." CHICAGO XXV is an album that the band should be proud of, not only well made but an outstanding holiday album as well. And for the first official Chicago album to spring forth from Chicago Records, Inc., it made a pretty good dent in the charts. Entering *Billboard* at Number 178 on November 28, 1998, the record raced to its peak position of Number 47 on December 12th.

And although it is not as avant-garde as STONE OF SISYPHUS (which still remains unreleased), it is filled with uncompromising musicianship and quality.

1998 was a busy year for Chicago. After recording the Christmas album, the band went on a full-blown summer tour with Hall & Oates and then hit the road on their own. Chicago spent the holiday season promoting the new album quite heavily, which seemed only natural, since they had become their own record label. Aside from constant touring, Chicago could be seen and heard on numerous radio and television stations across the country. The band was an integral part of the story line on a holiday episode of the soap opera *General Hospital*. Robert Lamm portrayed himself and was later joined by his bandmates. The group performed *If You Leave Me Now* and *Oh Come All Ye Faithful*.

CHICAGO XXVI

LIVE IN CONCERT

CRD 3026

Walter Parazaider ∾ Lee Loughnane ∾ James Pankow ∾ Tris Imboden ∾ Robert Lamm ∾ Jason Scheff ∾ Keith Howland ∾ Bill Champlin

The Ballet:
    Make Me Smile/
        So Much To Say...
    So Much To Give/
        Anxiety's Moment...
(I've Been) Searchin' So Long
Mongonucleosis
Hard Habit To Break
Call On Me
Feelin' Stronger Every Day

Just You 'N Me
Beginnings
Hard To Say I'm Sorry/
    Get Away
25 Or 6 To 4
Back To You
If I Should Lose You
(Your Love Keeps Lifting Me)
    Higher And Higher

CHICAGO XXVI was the band's last album released in the 20th century. Recorded live in Chicago, Atlantic City, and at the Foxwoods resort in Mashantucket, Connecticut, the album finds Chicago sounding as vital and energetic as ever. The album contains the entire "Ballet," as it is now known by the band, as well as nine other classic songs. There are three new ones as well, *Back To You, If I Should Ever Lose You,* and a remake of the old Jackie Wilson hit, *Higher And Higher,* with a lead vocal by the inimitable Michael McDonald.

With Keith Howland firmly in place, this is the best lineup Chicago has had since the original band. For CHICAGO XXVI, the band held fast to the traditional arrangements of the songs. Tris Imboden stayed true to Danny Seraphine's previous work, while bassist Jason Scheff, who usually refrains from playing Peter Cetera's recorded bass lines in favor of his own, showed admirable restraint here, paying homage to his predecessor. In fact, the whole band seems to have decided to usher in the new millennium by paying respect to and embracing their past. Most of it works, but there are some exceptions. *Call On Me* and *(I've Been) Searchin' So Long* don't translate well into Scheff's voice.

CHICAGO XXVI

Perhaps Cetera's stamp is too indelible on those, and anything else ends up sounding like a cover band's version. But some things actually work better. Scheff sounds much more at home with *Feelin' Stronger Every Day* than Cetera when he sang it in concert. Cetera always seemed to try to change up the melody too much . . . probably a necessary evil and a product of singing the same song for too many years. And Robert Lamm's sentimental reading of *Colour My World* leaves you wondering why he never sang it in the first place.

Of the three new studio recordings the band produced, *If I Should Lose You*, sung by Bill Champlin, has the most style and substance. (Oddly enough, no writing credits were given on this album.) *Back To You*, sung by Jason Scheff, was the first single to be released in January 2000, which James Pankow hoped would be so successful that Chicago could claim hits in five decades.

Through those five decades, many fans have remained loyal to the band. Robert Barbiero, a highly accomplished musician from Robert Lamm's hometown, Brooklyn, New York, fell in love with the band in the summer of 1972. "I went with my family up to Connecticut to visit relatives," remembers Barbiero, "and I was riding in the car when I heard *Saturday In The Park* on the radio. I thought, 'Wow, these guys are good. A rock and roll band with horns. Cool! I was only thirteeen years old and had only been playing the trumpet for about a year, but I was determined to learn the horn part so I could play along with the record." Thus began Robert's infatuation with Chicago. In high school, Barbiero formed a band called Hollywood, named for the song on CHICAGO VI. The band also featured Seth Rosenberg on guitar and vocals, who played on Chico DeBarge's 1999 release, THE GAME, and veteran L.A. bassist and Peter Cetera devotee, Joe Iaquinto, both of whom still remain close friends with Barbiero. "Hollywood," says Barbiero, "was a Chicago-wannabe band, but we took it pretty far. We played a lot of gigs and then started writing and recording our own material, which ultimately sounded like Chicago, too. We made a pretty good demo in 1976 that we were proud of, and I took it to my cousin, who had industry connections. He told us that we were making a big mistake by trying to follow in Chicago's footsteps and that we should stop immediately and concentrate on our own sound. We didn't listen and the band eventually broke up because we couldn't generate any real interest from the record companies."

The cousin that Barbiero speaks of is Michael Barbiero, who produced and engineered Blues Traveler's highly successful 1990 album, FOUR, which included their breakthrough hit single, *Runaround*. "Michael's got some heavy credits,"

FEELIN' STRONGER EVERY DAY

states Robert. "He's also worked with Counting Crows (1996's RECOVERING THE SATELLITES) and Guns 'N Roses (1987's huge hit album, APPETITE FOR DESTRUCTION). Maybe we shoulda listened to him!" Michael Barbiero has also produced, mixed, and/or engineered records for Mick Jagger, Madonna, Metallica, The Red Hot Chili Peppers, Aretha Franklin, Earth, Wind & Fire, and a slew of others. Robert's family tree also boasts the late Felix Pappalardi, legendary bassist and producer with the rock trio, Mountain. "Felix was a second cousin on my father's side," says Barbiero. Pappalardi also produced highly influential recordings for artists like Cream, Jack Bruce, Eric Clapton, Hot Tuna, and The Flock.

After Hollywood broke up, Robert did a short-lived road stint with Little Anthony, playing trumpet and piano. "I still play semi-professionally," says Robert. "My current band, Rave, performs at corporate functions and weddings and we do the occasional Chicago song. In fact, we worked up their arrangement of *Let It Snow* from the Christmas album, which I love." Barbiero finally got a chance to meet his heros in 1997. "They were performing at Jones Beach. A friend of mine is an entertainment reporter and she offered me tickets and backstage passes," he explains. "In fact, I called Joe Iaquinto, who was on the road in Green Bay, Wisconsin, and woke him up. I wanted him to tell me that I should sub out my gig so that I could go meet Chicago. I needed the validation. He told me that he would kill me if I didn't! It was great. The band sounded great, and I got to meet everyone. I even got to hang out and talk shop with Lee Loughnane. I kept hoping that Lee would have come down with something so that I could have played the show. I have all those horn parts down! I thoroughly enjoyed meeting all the guys, and I still love them and their music, new and old."

There in lies the enduring appeal of Chicago. The band still has a phalanx of devotees who come to see their concerts, cheering for the old songs and hoping to maybe one day see that rumored reunion that will see Peter Cetera and Danny Seraphine return to the fold. Then there is the other faction that adores the new band and will lap up anything and everything, especially the new material. These are the folks who fill the on-line chatrooms, debating Scheff vs. Cetera, Tris vs. Danny, and so on. And that is what makes Chicago great. That is why the band continues to work into the 21st century.

"No, we're not the band that recorded CHICAGO TRANSIT AUTHORITY," Robert Lamm remarks. "But we're a really good band and, in some ways, a better band. And yet it remains Chicago." As James Pankow remarks, "Let's

CHICAGO XXVI

face it, we've outlasted some of the buildings we've played in."

"How it has occurred that we've remained a vital part of the musical landscape over all these years is a mystery to me," says Robert Lamm. "We're still chasing the elusive idea that we have to make that really great recording. On an album level, that's what motivates us."

With Chicago as alive as ever, one thing is for certain, no matter how many guitar players or bass players or drummers or singers pass through the door, the heart and soul of this great band, the music, will continue to make us smile. And for this, to quote Terry Kath, "we do thank the Lord."

ACKNOWLEDGMENTS

The author thanks Kristine and Kevin Iaquinto, Maireid Sullivan, Rob Barbiero, Jere Mendelsohn, John Einarson, Greg Prestopino, Seth Rosenberg, Karen Simpson, Bruce Becker, Kevin Knutsen, Mark Gianchetti, Jeff Ganz, The Landers, Julia, Jarred, Kirsten and Kurt, Kiki Ebsen, Chris Ralles, Mark Goldenberg, Bill Champlin (for his honesty and candor), Louis "Fred" Ohland (for the computer), Ramon Alarcon (for all the "Sons of Champlin" albums), several Deep Throats... and a very special thanks to Joe Iaquinto and Ben Kettlewell, without whom this book could not have been written. Wayland Langley White, you are loved and remembered. This book is dedicated to the memory of my parents, who were taken much too soon.

SOURCES

The author acknowledges the following sources of quotations from Chicago band members and associates, in addition to the personal interviews he conducted with Bill Champlin, Bob Ludwig, Mark Goldenberg, Kiki Ebsen, Joe Iaquinto, and Robert Barbiero, as well as several other members of the band who requested anonymity: Joel Leach (*Wind Player*, Jan/Feb 1988); Melinda Newman (*Modern Recording & Music*, July 1985); Betsy Pickle (*Knoxville News Sentinel*, November 6, 1986), David Veitch (*Calgary Sun*, March 1, 1996); Paul Grein (*Billboard*, January 26, 1985); Dennis Hunt (*Los Angeles Times*, June 20, 1982); Baker Rorick (*Relic Magazine*); Jon Young (*Rolling Stone*); Robyn Flans (*Modern Drummer*, December 1995); Ian Blair (*Music Connection*, August 1985); John Swenson (*Rolling Stone*, November 3, 1977); Chris Jordan (*Home News Tribune*, November 1998); Edwin Miller (*Seventeen Magazine*, December 1973); Chuck Taylor (*Billboard*, 1998); Lester Bangs (*Rolling Stone*, March 18, 1971); R. Hohman (*Down Beat*, 1974); Mort Goode (Liner Notes to "Andre Kostelanetz Plays Chicago"); Walter Tunis; Dan Kening; Jeff DeWester; Mike Quigley; Henry Kujawa; *mm* magazine; *Bass Frontiers*; *People Magazine*; *Creem Magazine* (Feb 1976); and *Circus*. Special credit is due to William Ruhlmann for his excellent liner notes for "Group Portrait" and William James Guercio for liner notes for "Chicago II." Every effort has been made to attribute sources; however, if any have been inadvertently omitted, please contact the publisher so that credit can be given in subsequent editions.